All You Need Is

LOVE

to Dismantle an

ATOMIC BOMB

All You Need Is

LOVE

to Dismantle an

ATOMIC BOMB

How the Beatles and U2 Changed the World

Todd McFliker

continuum

NEW YORK • LONDON

2007

The Continuum International Publishing Group Inc
80 Maiden Lane, New York, NY 10038

The Continuum International Publishing Group Ltd
The Tower Building, 11 York Road, London SE1 7NX
www.continuumbooks.com

Printed in the United States of America

Library of Congress Cataloging-in-Publication Data

McFliker, Todd.
   All you need is love to dismantle an atomic bomb : how the Beatles and U2 changed the world / Todd McFliker.
        p. cm.
   Includes bibliographical references and index.
   ISBN-13: 978-0-8264-2776-2 (pbk. : alk. paper)
   ISBN-10: 0-8264-2776-6 (pbk. : alk. paper)
1. Beatles. 2. U2 (Musical group) 3. Rock musicians—England—Biography.
4. Rock musicians—Ireland—Biography. 5. Rock music—Social aspects.
6. Rock music—History and criticism. I. Title.

ML421.B4M26 2007
782.42166092'2—dc22
[B]

                              2007009275

Continuum is a member of Green Press Initiative, a nonprofit program dedicated to supporting publishers in their efforts to reduce their use of fiber obtained from endangered forests. We have elected to print this title on 30% postconsumer waste recycled paper. For more information, go to www.greenpressinitiative.org.

For
Ms. Mary Carter

"Take a sad song and make it better."

"What you don't have, you don't need it now.
What you don't know, you can feel it somehow."
It really is a beautiful day.

Thank you to Dr. David Jaffe for coming up with the idea and allowing me to write the *Beatles' Revolution* manuscript for my practicum. Thank you to Dr. Erika Grodzki for guiding me through the process. Mom and Dad, *muchas gracias* for your unconditional support. Thank you to Sean McCloskey and *RAG Magazine* for the phenomenal photography of U2 and Sir Paul.

Contents

Introduction

TRUE, IT WAS BEFORE MY TIME, but the Beatles were the sociological and cultural phenomenon of the twentieth century. In the 1960s, the musical messiahs from Liverpool pioneered a new fulfilling era of music based on the simple concepts of love, peace, and enlightenment. Seventy-three million television viewers witnessed the Beatles' first live performance in the United States. For the next six years, baby boomers experienced Beatlemania daily on TV, in movies, on the radio, and in printed interviews. The most popular, repeatedly covered, influential, and enduring rock group of all time made rock and roll an artistic medium with recognizable images and idols. Although the Beatles have not recorded an album since 1969, the four lads remain the best-selling artists in the United States to date.

In the mid-1980s, I was more preoccupied with the music of Van Halen than that of my parents' generation. Yes, I was hip to "Twist and Shout" when Ferris Bueller sang the number, but I was nowhere near calling myself a Beatles fan. In the same period of time, U2 was reaching global fame with *The Joshua Tree*, and "With or Without You" was the hottest thing on MTV; you remember, back when they actually showed music videos. I still wasn't much of an admirer, but both my older brother and sister loved the popular band from Ireland. A few years later, "Desire" was aired just prior to *Rattle and Hum*'s release in theaters. I was immediately hooked. Listening to the record's introductory song, "Helter Skelter," I got a history lesson on Charles Manson and the Beatles. In the early '90s, I was in high school when *Achtung Baby* and Zoo TV conquered the planet. The singles "The Fly" and "Mysterious Ways" immediately won me over. Their Zoo TV tour in 1992–1993 was a multimedia extravaganza like I had never before experienced.

Reported as the biggest band on the planet since the 1980s, U2 has dominated the industry for a quarter-century by marketing the Beatles' theme of love throughout the media. The four friends out of Dublin have sold over one hundred million records worldwide. A rock concert was suddenly more than the band simply reproducing their latest record onstage. The show set a new level for massive concert productions around the world. U2's CDs, musical productions, and public appearances in the political spotlight still remain momentous in the new millennium.

Arguably the best albums of their time periods, the Beatles' 1967 release, *Sgt. Pepper's Lonely Hearts Club Band*, is directly compared with U2's modern masterpiece, *Achtung Baby*, from 1991. While the recording of *Sgt. Pepper's* was too highly technical to hit the road with at the time, *Achtung Baby*, with its Zoo TV tour nearly thirty years later, was the largest, loudest, most costly and technically ambitious rock show to ever tour the globe.

Printed reports of both the Beatles' and U2's legendary concerts are examined thoroughly to show differences and comparisons in different media outlets. The Beatles' US tours in 1964 and 1965 changed American culture, as the youth were led in new directions in music, clothing, hairstyles, and vocabulary. In 1965, a Beatles concert at New York City's Shea Stadium broke loose of all records for rock-show attendance, attracting over 55,600 spectators.

Since 1991's Zoo TV, U2 has presented rock and roll as a spectacle in different nations' most enormous stadiums, utilizing technical, aesthetic, and theatrical devices. Readers may observe different views on white-skinned, jelly-bean-pelting Beatles fans, as well as a variety of write-ups discussing U2's performances to an older and more respectful crowd of diverse listeners. The two bands' amount of time on stage, quality of sound, and audience participation are also compared. Both the Beatles and U2 have undoubtedly expanded society's expectations of live performances with their unforgettable rock concerts.

When U2 released *Zooropa* in 1993, I joined the masses in being turned off of the band. They had taken their electronic experimentation a step too far. I felt the same way about *Pop* in '97. I recall seeing the PopMart tour with my brother-in-law. We were both disappointed. In fact, Bono pleaded with the audience in Miami to stick with U2 through their avant-garde stage. Thousands missed the melodic material from 1987's *The Joshua Tree* and the fast-paced rhythms of *Achtung Baby*, as well as the excitement of their concerts. Coincidently, that's the same period of time when I stumbled upon a life-altering CD. I was an undergraduate studying English when I picked up the Beatles *Anthology 2* at a used-record shop, CD Connection, in Boca Raton. *Anthology 2* contains countless classics that I had never heard before, from "You've Got to Hide Your Love Away" and different outtakes of "I'm Only Sleeping" to the "Sgt. Pepper's Lonely Hearts Club Band" reprise. The double-disc release from 1996 turned me into an immediate fan of the Fab Four. Two other *Anthologies* eventually joined my collection, as well as the DVD set. With each new purchase, I was blown away at the new findings, the extraordinary music, and true-to-life messages I found in the Beatles' material.

Bono felt a similar experience with John Lennon and penned a direct response to the Beatle's "God," recorded in 1970. Bono wrote "God Part II," a more poetic pop song, using symbolism, quoting modern-day journalists, and mocking himself. John helped make rock and roll an acceptable medium in a handful of cultures around the world. Utilizing his unquestionable talents in the 1960s, Lennon wrote, performed, and recorded material based on love, justice, equality, integrity, and risk in order to better mankind. While John's legacy continues to shine on, Bono is the media's most successful activist of all time. U2's pop star has continually admitted he would not have a role to play if it were not for previous icons, such as the Beatles. In the 1980s and '90s, the Irish boys performed in Band Aid, Farm Aid, Live Aid, and "A Conspiracy of Hope" tours. Bono also traveled to Ethiopia and spent six weeks working with children in an orphanage. Today, Bono's resume includes multiple activist groups and charities. U2's front man was nominated for a Nobel Peace Prize in 2003 but lost the honor to an Iranian human rights advocate. Bono was up for the award again in 2005 and 2006.

Along with their infamous "Bed-In," John and Yoko Ono performed a series of rock concerts around the world as a political statement of peace and love. Taking things a step further, Bono has met directly with President George W. Bush and was named as a potential candidate to lead the World Bank in 2005. A few months later, *Time* magazine named Bono as co-Person of the Year, on the twenty-five-year anniversary of John Lennon's murder. In fact, Bono has admitted that his role in society only exists because of the four Englishmen. Without the Beatles' and U2's revolutionary music, godly poetry, timeless performances, cultural influences, and political involvement, the entertainment industry, including my own professional career in music journalism, would not have evolved on such a profound magnitude across the universe.

2

The Beatles' Revolution

ALMOST WITHOUT QUESTION, the Beatles were the greatest power in popular music the world has ever seen. It all started in the 1950s, when Elvis Presley's distinctly American music style, rock and roll, drifted across the ocean to the United Kingdom. Artists such as Chuck Berry, Little Richard, and Buddy Holly made a lasting impression on the English youth as well. The new concept was that white men could sing like black men. British teenagers began imitating this music, using the guitar, washboard, and tea-chest bass as instruments. By the middle of the 1960s, the Beatles had become the sociological and cultural phenomenon of the twentieth century. They were the groundbreaking pioneers of a new, fulfilling era of music based on the concepts of love, peace, and enlightenment.

In June of 1957, Paul McCartney met John Lennon, the leader of a rock band called the Quarrymen, as they both attended Liverpool's Quarry Bank High School. After hearing Paul play guitar, John asked him to join his group. Before long,

Paul introduced John to another musician, George Harrison. John quickly asked the talented guitarist to join the Quarrymen as well. In July of 1962, the Quarrymen, by this time called the Beatles, fired their original drummer and hired Ringo Starr to handle the percussion.

John Winston Lennon was the "brainy Beatle." Extremely intelligent and candid, he was known as the spokesman for the band. Born on October 9, 1940, John grew up on jazz and authored his first fiction book, *Sport, Speed and Illustrated*, at the age of seven. He was the only Beatle to be married.[1] John has claimed that his life changed when he first heard Elvis Presley's *Heartbreak Hotel*. His mother bought him a secondhand guitar and taught him old banjo chords.

James Paul McCartney was known as the "cute Beatle." Born in 1942, his dad played the piano regularly at home. Before long, Paul received a guitar as a gift and the instrument never left his sight.

George Harrison has been dubbed the "quiet Beatle." Despite being the most flamboyant dresser of all the Beatles, the youngest member of the combo was usually shy and reserved in the public spotlight. Playing guitar since he was fourteen years old, George, as well as the other Beatles, grew up on "skiffle," or hillbilly music. Paul's younger brother, Michael, recalls George wearing his hair long years before anybody else in Liverpool did.

Finally, Ringo Starr, the so-called "funny Beatle," came on board to complete the quartet. Ringo earned his nickname by wearing several rings on his fingers.[2] Yet all of the jewelry on his hands never slowed down the nimble drummer, whose real name is Richard Starkey.

The band's name came from John's admiration for an American group, Buddy Holly and the Crickets, sparking the idea of insects, or "beetles," into his head. The young musician, always clever with language, decided to spell it "Beatles" to make it a pun; as in the insect, as well as representing the band's heavy musical "beat."

The Beatles' arrival on *The Ed Sullivan Show* made TV history, introducing the United States to the future leaders of the entertainment industry. In February of 1964, over three thousand hysterical Beatlemaniacs greeted the Fab Four at New York's newly renamed

Kennedy Airport, just prior to the band's appearance on *Sullivan*. The Neilson ratings indicated that 43 percent of all TV sets in the country were tuned to Sullivan's variety show to witness John, Paul, George, and Ringo perform.[3] It was reported that the crime rate among American teenagers dropped to virtually zero that night. Offering wit, charm, love, youth, and happiness, the Beatles' arrival in the States was instrumental in picking up the overall morale of the country, stunned by the November 1963 assassination of President John Kennedy, and in doctoring the culture with *the so-called* second British Invasion. The ambitious boys from the British Isles were the most phenomenal thing to hit show business since the "talkies." *Rolling Stone* reporter David Fricke explained, "In one hour and five songs, the hottest rock act in Britain became the biggest pop group in America, immediately transforming the character and future of a generation."[4]

The Beatles used the media in a remarkable fashion, possessing and caressing their audience with a quick wit, which was showcased endlessly on television, in movies, on the radio, and in printed interviews. But most importantly, their legacy is due to their timeless music. The most popular, most covered, influential, and enduring group of all time made rock and roll an artistic medium with recognizable images and idols. Fans went ballistic for the Beatles, fainting and tearing at the clothes on their bodies. The music messiahs from Liverpool swept up the youthful hopes of entire generations. For over three decades, Beatlemania has been spreading to the masses.

Although the four Beatles have not recorded an album since 1969, fan pursuit of the group remains high in the third millennium. Their back catalog has been selling millions of units a year. From their first legendary American TV appearance in 1964, to a number of feature-length films, to *Rolling Stone*'s countless articles, to the millions of albums sold decades after a deranged fan shot and killed Lennon in 1980, the Beatles' power with the media has remained unmatched for forty years.

There was not one day during the latter half of the 1960s that there was not some kind of story about the Beatles on television, in the newspapers, or on the radio. The baby boom generation went nuts over the band, buying literally millions of Beatles records. The four fellas were certainly wittier, while singing more grounded lyrics than preceding rock stars in America, such as Elvis, Ricky Nelson, or Pat Boone. Unlike those previously mentioned US artists, the Beatles wrote their own material, and painted pictures with lyrics, expanding boundaries around the world.

By 1963, the Beatles had swept all of Europe. In early 1964, "I Want to Hold Your Hand" was number one on the US Top 100. Two months later, the Beatles had become the dominant force in the US music market; they occupied the first five places in the American *Billboard* magazine singles charts. During the first week in April, the top five consisted of "Can't Buy Me Love," "Twist and Shout," "She Loves You," "I Want to Hold Your Hand," and "Please Please Me." This phenomenal feat was a first for rock and roll, and the record still stands in the twenty-first century.

They also occupied the first six positions on the Australian charts with a completely different set of singles one week prior. By the summer, the hits were coming faster than ever from across the pond. Before the Beatles led their 1960s British Invasion, the popularity of European acts was confined to their own continent. Before the American arrival of the Beatles, there were many English artists who were a smash at home but died when they came to the States.

Many fans who experienced the Beatles' live performances in any part of the world describe the group as listless and unremarkable. After all, the Beatles often appeared as black atoms to these concertgoers, hidden behind wire-mesh fencing two hundred feet away from the nearest fan. Their voices could not be heard, and each band member appeared to be no more than a speck to the spectators. The whirlwind of concerts, films, TV appearances, press conferences, and photo shoots took its strain. The Beatles decided to retire from performing live shows, and they played their last concert together on August 29, 1966.

The boys also starred on international movie screens. Thanks to their global influence, England had also become a fashion center in the mid-'60s, as these British artists influenced the visual appearance of the world's youth. First, Americans mimicked the boys' mop-top hairstyle, in contrast to the almost military short-back-and-sides look of previous years, along with the Beatles' Cuban-heeled boots.

The Beatles sang more thoughtful and grown-up lyrics in numbers such as "All You Need Is Love," "Nowhere Man," and "Norwegian Wood" than many of the world's preceding rock stars. In later years, the boys' lyrics got even more sophisticated. Their inspiring songs, such as the powerful "A Day in the Life" and "Lucy in the Sky With Diamonds," depicted real-life social awareness. The complexity of their lyrics obviously influenced bands, such as U2 and America's Jane's Addiction, around the globe for several decades.

Due to the greater population, the Beatles' record sales were substantially higher in America than they were in the band's homeland. In the year 1964, *A Hard Day's Night* sold $1 million worth of records in only four days. The album enjoyed fifty-one weeks on the US Top 100 chart but only forty-three on the UK chart.[5] Meanwhile, the cinema verité film *A Hard Day's Night* was shot in black and white over a seven-week period. At that time, the editing technique of cutting the images in time to the musical beat was considered radical. Production time was so short because the studio foolishly believed that Beatlemania would not last past the summer of '64. The next year, the *Help!* LP brought in over $3 million in the States and was in the Top 100 for forty-four weeks, three weeks longer than in the United Kingdom's. In 1965, *Rubber Soul* made over $1 million in nine days and remained fifty-nine weeks on the US chart and forty-seven on the United Kingdom's.[6] *Revolver* earned over a million dollars, spending seventy-seven weeks in the States' Top 100, and forty-six in the UK's chart.

Sgt. Pepper's Lonely Hearts Club Band was somewhat different from the rest of the Beatles' records, as it actually experienced better sales in the United Kingdom than in the States. After sitting at number one for fifteen weeks and spending a total of 175 weeks on the charts, the album made over $11 million in the United States.[7] Meanwhile, *Sgt. Pepper's* spent 198 weeks on the UK chart, retaining the top position for twenty-seven weeks. With the White Album, the Beatles sales returned to their old pattern, selling almost $2 million in its first week of release in America. The record spent 155 weeks on the US chart and twenty-four on the UK's. The Fab Four's last two albums had similar sales in 1969; *Yellow Submarine* spent twenty-five weeks on the US chart and eleven on the UK listing, while *Abbey Road* spent 129 in the US top 100 and ninety-two on the UK chart. All in all, the Beatles sold 106 million records worldwide before they disbanded in 1970.[8]

In 1968, a photograph of Lennon and Yoko Ono, both nude, on *Rolling Stone* magazine's first-anniversary issue cover was a political bombshell for the time. The idea of a couple so famous and so physically average standing completely naked for the world to see was quite revolutionary, symbolizing peace and love in the turbulent time.

"Helter Skelter" is one of the Beatles' most historically important tracks. Released in November of 1968, on the untitled Beatles record known today as the White Album, one crazed fan found particular cynicism in the Fab Four's timeless work. In 1969, Charles Manson became one of history's most infamous villains, claiming to have been inspired by the band's sounds and lyrics.

Born in the 1930s to an unwed mother, Manson was a mind-controlling psychopath who sent his brainwashed followers, known as "the Family," into the Hollywood hills to slaughter a handful of innocent victims in the summer of 1969. He believed that John, Paul, George, and Ringo were actually the four horsemen from the book of Revelation, and that they were telling him to spark a race war between blacks and whites.

Lennon once reflected on the Manson killings, in December of 1970, claiming that the fiasco had nothing to do with the Beatles, and that Manson was crazy. Diametrically, Manson was a huge fan of the Fab Four. He claimed to have heard "clues" and "messages" in their albums. As a result, drugged members of the Family were "being brainwashed by Manson's hypnotic biblical exhortations and metaphors gleaned from Beatles songs."[9] His delusions were not unlike the 1970s' notorious murderers the Son of Sam, David Berkowitz, who believed that a dog was his master, and the later Unabomber, Ted Kaczynski, who went on a seventeen-year bombing campaign. Kaczynski thought that society was trying to control individuals' emotions via electrodes, genetic engineering, and the development of superhuman computers.

There was "something in the way" Manson spoke to his Family. Similar to Adolf Hitler addressing mass audiences, calling for the German people to resist "the yoke of Jews and Communists," or even the "charming" Ted Bundy in the 1970s, Manson often appeared a remarkably likable character. Perhaps it was the LSD, but he touched his followers' hearts, earning an unquestionable loyalty. In the book *Manson in His Own Words*, Manson explains, "Everything I said seemed to impress those around me. It didn't matter that I was an ex-felon, or that I could barely write my name. What mattered was that I could make those I talked to feel comfortable with themselves. My . . . words affected lots of people."[10]

In the summer of 1969, the members of Manson's cult in Los Angeles followed his orders and committed brutal murder. The bizarre homicides were committed with pure savagery, as each victim was stabbed dozens of times with ordinary kitchen forks and knives. Blood was used to scrawl out messages referring to the Beatles, such as PIGGY and RISE, and the misspelled HEALTER SKELTER on the refrigerator. The leader himself was not actually present at the massacre.

According to Manson's teachings, the blacks would rise up and slaughter the whites. In his delusions of grandeur, he believed his brainwashed Family would hide in a so-called Hole, adopted from Hopi Indians' religion. When the Family emerged from the Hole, Manson would be seen as Christ, despite the swastika tattoo on his forehead, and would take power over the earth.[11]

In metaphors and symbols, the songs on the White Album underscored all that Manson had been teaching. "Blackbird" was interpreted as a call to the black man to rise up against the whites.

Beatles sketch, *by Nic Luciano*

"Piggies" was about the members of society who deserved to die. "Revolution 9" was a direct reference to the final book of the Bible, Revelation 9, also known as the Apocalypse Plan. Finally, "Helter Skelter" was the name of their mission, rather than a slide in an amusement park, as the English use the term.

"Helter Skelter is confusion," Manson explained in 1970. "Confusion is coming down fast. . . . It is not my conspiracy. It is not my music. I hear what it relates. It says, 'Rise!' It says, 'Kill!' Why blame it on me? I didn't write the music."[12] In the book of Revelation, verse 3 states: "Out of the smoke came forth locusts upon the earth; and power was given them." Delusional Manson believed that the "locusts" were in fact "beetles," or the world-renowned Beatles. The book also refers to the locusts having faces like men and "hair of women," which can be seen as references to the Fab Four. Their "breastplates of iron" could be interpreted as electric guitars.

In the 1970s, one-time member of Manson's Family, Charles Watson recalled that the Beatles' music had nothing to do with the murders. Their songs were merely misinterpreted by Manson, who developed a false teaching of Beatles' music. Most English-speaking youngsters of the following generation recognize "Helter Skelter" from U2's cover version of the song off of their 1988 *Rattle and Hum* record.

By the end of the 1960s, the Beatles were perceived as larger than life. Yet, their recording sessions were full of disagreements and disappointments, and rarely would band members record music together in the studio. On January 19, 1971, Paul McCartney petitioned England's High Court to dissolve the Beatles' business partnership.

Before the Beatles led the charge, a British act's popularity was generally confined to Europe. There were many English artists who were a smash at home but died when they came to the States, explained Capitol Records executive Dave Dexter Jr. Some American artists had to base themselves in Britain before gaining recognition to successfully conquer the States, as was the case with Jimi Hendrix.

There had been merely a small percentage of rock-and-roll artists on the charts immediately prior to the British Invasion. In the 1960s, the baby boomers were in their teens and were beginning to control the world's media by mass consumption. Also, when the music industry first started making Beatles records, there were very few other things for adolescents, particularly twelve- to fifteen-year-olds, to spend their money on. There was a lack of competition in the global music industry's market. True, the English bands had great promotion, such as the *Sullivan Show*, but raw talent paved the way to fame and fortune for each of them.

Before the Beatles led the British Invasion, rock-and-roll music was looked down on by many media outlets in the States. The exciting spell that the British groups cast on American youth was sensational. The Invasion inspired America's youth to form more groups, rather than perform as solo artists. A prime example is the Byrds, who were once labeled "the American Beatles," heavily influenced by the unified smoothness of the British style.

Some concept albums from the States that are comparable to *Sgt. Pepper's* include the Beach Boys' 1963 *Little Deuce Coupe*, featuring

Pencil sketching, *by Daniel Camilli*

various car-related songs celebrating America's culture. In 1966, the band released *Pet Sounds*, a classic autobiographical work about love and life. The following year, the Jimi Hendrix Experience recorded *Axis: Bold as Love*, the tale of one man's journey for true love on the earth's axis. The year brought the Who's *Tommy*, the tale of a deaf, dumb, and blind pinball wizard. The same year, the Kinks sang about a middle-aged man who gradually loses touch with society in their concept album *Arthur; or, The Decline and Fall of the British Empire*.

The worldwide success of *Sgt. Pepper's* psychedelic rock led to the emergence of music associated with the use of hallucinogenic drugs, such as lysergic acid diethylamide, a.k.a. LSD. With the new "acid rock," an antiestablishment orientation of the youth culture developed worldwide, particularly strong among antiwar, peace-loving hippies in San Francisco. Musicians on both sides of the Atlantic experimented with long, improvised jams. The new jams emphasized spontaneity, and communitarian values became popular around the globe. Such psychedelic music is not nearly as popular in the new millennium's global cultures, as acid rock has grown out-of-date, and the psychedelic drug culture is now frowned upon.

Hand in hand with the music invasion, British stage musicals such as *Oliver!* garnered worldwide fame in the 1960s as well. In 1968, Stanley Kubrick changed the world's motion picture industry with his homebuilt special effects in *2001: A Space Odyssey*. An Oxford professor, J.R.R. Tolkien, gained global fame for his mystifying novels. As noted, England had also become the fashion center of the world in the mid-'60s, as British artists influenced the visual appearance of the globe's youth, particularly in hairstyle and footwear. The military style in men's clothing was later popularized by Hendrix and Mick Jagger.

In the same decade, there were few articles in the States that dealt with rock and roll. After all, *Rolling Stone*, the music magazine out of San Francisco, was not founded until 1967. However, the English already had a wide selection of newspapers to choose from, including *Melody Maker*, *Sounds*, and *Record Mirror*, while their glossy-magazine selection included *Circus*, *Cream*, and the Australian *Go-Set*. Each of the periodicals was imported to the States at a high cost for the consumers.

Of all the British rock groups, only the Rolling Stones offered a consistent challenge to the Beatles. The rhythm-and-blues artists out of London portrayed a bad-boy image that was the reverse of the lads from Liverpool. John Lennon once lamented that the Stones wound up with the snarling-rocker image with songs such as "Satisfaction," "Under My Thumb," and "Paint It, Black," whereas the American press made his band out to look like mama's boys.

The Stones' 1968 album, *Beggars Banquet*, reached $1 million in sales in the States, a huge number at the time, but only one-fifth of that in Great Britain. One of the LP's numbers, "Sympathy for the Devil," was obviously written for an American audience, as the lyrics ask, "Who killed the Kennedys? . . . After all, it was you and me." The same album also features lyrics for everyday laborers, such as those in "Factory Girl."

Throughout the 1960s, the Who made a continuous bid to be considered one of England's top bands by singing directly to their generation of boomers. The band added an ambitious dimension to rock culture by writing a rock opera about alienation. *Tommy* is the story of a disabled child who expresses himself and grows famous by becoming a pinball wizard. The play has been staged globally by a number of opera companies for four decades.

The Who's manic drummer, Keith Moon, introduced the idea of the explosive-style drummer to rock and served as a role model to thousands of Americans, such as Motley Crue's Tommy Lee. Meanwhile, Moon's bandmates refined the art of smashing guitars and speakers onstage, as later seen in the States by Nirvana and Pearl Jam in the 1990s. One British newspaper printed an article with the heading "The Who—Richest Vandalists in the World."[13]

Like the Beatles, the Who was quite creative and extremely innovative in their recording techniques. As Leonard Michaels points out in the *Rolling Stone* Beatles anniversary issue, "Before George Lucas, they were doing special effects."[14] The band would record their songs from a microphone at the other end of a corridor, using incredible amounts of compression to make symbols sound like a steam engine. Each of the recording tricks is commonplace inside a twenty-first-century studio in America. In 1967, an army brat from Seattle—in part inspired by the rough voice of Bob Dylan—who did not need any tricks in the studio, flew to England to record his psychedelic, left-handed guitar playing. Consequently, Jimi Hendrix stunned the British and within months, his records crashed the American scene with epics such as "Voodoo Chile." Almost forty years later, he is still considered the greatest electric guitarist ever.

Herman's Hermits, featuring their strong British accents, had eighteen US hits in the '60s. A couple of the band's number one hits were "Mrs Brown You've Got a Lovely Daughter" and "I'm Into Something Good." Similarly, the Kinks were one of the most influential bands of the British Invasion with nine American hits in the mid-'60s, including "You Really Got Me" and "Lola." The Kinks drew heavily from traditional pop, and incorporated elements of folk and blues in their tunes.

On the subject of the blues, London introduced the world's next gods of rock, Led Zeppelin, by the end of the decade. The band begged, borrowed, and stole from American blues legends, such as Otis Redding and Howlin' Wolf, creating a sensation with their brash performances. The singles "Whole Lotta Love" and "Black Dog" were each revelations of sound, and their timeless hits include the most requested radio song ever, "Stairway to Heaven," and "Ramble On," which drew lyrics from Tolkien's mysterious novels. Zeppelin became the biggest band of the following decade, releasing eight studio albums and popularizing the stadium rock concert. Zeppelin performed over 130 concerts to clubs, colleges, and stadiums in one year, conquering the United Kingdom, France, Scandinavia, the United States, and Canada. However, the band was treated quite cruelly by the American media, who mercilessly panned their LPs, until the mid-1970s. Regardless, Zeppelin has been influential and inspirational to countless American bands, ranging from White Snake to Stone Temple Pilots.

In a book from the late 1990s about Led Zeppelin, Chris Welch compares the Kings of Stadium Rock to other English acts: "Zeppelin may not have captured the public's affection in the same way as the Beatles or the Rolling Stones, and they may not have been as flashy as the Who or the Jimi Hendrix Experience, but there was a monumental strength about the . . . crew that over-whelmed all opposition."[15]

Yet English rock did not swamp the charts, as American artists continued to hold sway. During the 1960s, less than 10 percent of US record sales were British, and no more than two dozen English acts had hits in the States, never overcoming the Americans' dominance. The majority of these groups had a few hits in the mid-'60s but lacked staying power.

British bands of the 1960s were inventive, experimental, funny, and charming, while their music was often extraordinary. It has been forty years since the music crossed the Atlantic and the

English bands are still better than the less sincere artists performing in today's money-hungry and prestigious market. The music is certainly more fun, too.

There has never been an equivalent to the Beatles and the 1960s British Invasion, nor will there ever be. Such a phenomenon could not happen in today's market. Teens often push music aside, favoring mobile phones and computer games. At the same time, these consumers readily access Internet downloads and music file sharing, taking millions of dollars away from the industry that the Beatles once dominated.

Each of the 1960s music messiahs from England swept up the youthful hopes of an entire generation of Americans, as well as millions of others around the world. The Beatles, in particular, used the media in a remarkable fashion, possessing and caressing, inciting and inviting consumers' eyes and ears with pure talent, wit, and humor. They won over foreign audiences with their quick wits with the media. Perhaps the global fame of the States' greatest bands, such as Jane's Addiction, Nirvana, and Pearl Jam, would not have existed on such a wide scale, if at all, if it were not for the British legends invading the American culture in the 1960s.

3

U2

FOUR PEOPLE,
FOUR INDIVIDUALS,
FOUR FRIENDS

U2'S FRONT MAN, BONO, used to open the band's live performances by explaining that they are not another English band passing through. For one thing, U2 is Irish. Inspired by the gallant gestures of the 1960s, U2 has sold over one hundred million records throughout the world. The band has dominated the entertainment industry for a quarter century by marketing the Beatles' theme of love into albums, concerts, movies, and books.

U2's quarter-of-a-century history greatly exceeds the Beatles' six-year stint. They have all been directly inspired by the magical sounds of the Stones, the Clash, and the Beatles. In fact, the first record that Bono connected with was "I Want to Hold Your Hand" when he was four years old. The Irish band got together in 1976 and drew global fame in the mid-1980s. The members of U2 began performing in Dublin's parking lots at ages fifteen and sixteen, since none of the boys were old enough to get into bars or clubs. Their original name was Feedback, followed by the Hype. The boys chose the name U2 to be indistinct and avoid being categorized, as a U2 was a military plane created for the cold war. Bono once dreamed of getting Lennon to produce a U2 record. In 2000, Bono told Robert Hilburn of the *Los Angeles Times* that while the Beatles "wrote the book on tunes," it was John who penned the influential book on "revealing your soul."[1]

In the 1970s, America's pop stars from Ireland consisted of the Blades, Astral Weeks, Thin Lizzy, and legendary Van Morrison. In the *Out of Ireland* documentary from 2003, Van Morrison declared, "U2 created the Irish music industry. It certainly wasn't there before."[2]

Drummer Larry Mullen Jr., now in his mid-forties, effectively started U2 at Dublin's Mount Temple Comprehensive School. Larry posted a want ad for musicians on the school bulletin board in 1976. Before long, the four got together and set out to be the Beatles of their generation. "I had two days of glory when I was telling people what to do," Larry explained in 1983. "Then Bono came in and that was the end. He took it from there."[3]

Losing his mother at a young age is a tragedy Larry has in common with John Lennon, Paul McCartney, and Bono. When Bono was fourteen, his mother suffered a lethal stroke at her father's funeral. Larry and Bono have always been opposites in the personality department. Bono is always game to experiment with new "ideas, fads, impulses, innovation, and rationalization."[4] Meanwhile, Larry is the conservative member of the band. The two work well off one another, as Bono inspires Larry to experiment. Likewise, Larry sometimes has to talk some sense into the singer's outrageous and futile ideas.

Bono is a self-proclaimed "egomaniac" and "naughty pop star."[5] Born as Paul Hewson on May 10, 1960, Bono got his name from childhood friends. Bono Vox means *beautiful voice*, as well as being the name of a local hearing-aid store in Dublin. U2's notorious front man is married. He tied the knot with his high school sweetheart, Ali, in 1982, and they have four children.

"I was eleven when John Lennon blew my mind," Bono explained to reporter Anthony De Curtis in 2000. Music meant everything to the young man in the '60s, and he knew he wanted a career inside the entertainment industry. With time and practice, Bono established a distinct singing voice with an Irish flavor.[6] In 1996, Larry accused Bono of having an identity crisis. The singer retorted with accusations of not knowing how to improvise. He pointed out Larry's haircut, which has not changed in two decades. Bono admitted, "Yes, I sometimes fail, but at least I'm willing to experiment."[7]

The Edge, U2's timeless guitarist, is a middle-aged father of three girls. He is known as the most serious member of the band and has always been soft-spoken. Both Bono and the Edge were given their stage names by a group of neighborhood friends in Dublin. Bono once referred to the Edge as "a girl with a mustache. . . . He drives a second-hand BMW, which he keeps strictly to the speed limit. . . . He has only . . . been called 'Mr. Edge' when checking into hotels."[8] Square or not, *Rolling Stone* declared the Edge number twenty-four in its "100 Greatest Guitarists of All Time." The Beatles' George Harrison was named number twenty-one.[9]

Adam Clayton is U2's bass player who moved from London to Dublin at age five. Being the youngest member of the band by a year or two, he is also known to be extremely sardonic, despite his gray hair and bookish spectacles. The black sheep of the band was once engaged briefly to supermodel Naomi Campbell and missed a gig in 1993 because he was too drunk to play. Today the bass player is still on the wagon. "Adam doesn't drink. . . . We've had some pretty good games of Scrabble," Bono explained in 2004.[10]

By the 1980s, Adam convinced manager Paul McGuinness to join the U2 outfit. After earning a local following in Dublin, as well as winning a talent show, U2 was given a record deal by the Irish affiliate of CBS. The band recorded a three-song demo record but made no commitments to the label.

When creating music, U2 reworked the Beatles' four-man lineup and simultaneously meshed punk and heavy metal into their unique sound. The rock bands of the 1970s, such as the Jeff Beck Group, Derek and the Dominos, and Led Zeppelin, all grew from the Jimi Hendrix model: one guitar leading with showy solos, while the bass and drum backed it up. However, U2 takes after the 1960s model, exemplified by the Beatles and the Who, with instruments in virtually equal proportions, not entailing flashy guitar solos.

According to Niall Stokes of the Irish magazine *Hot Press*, U2 first started performing as a very theatrical group, with Bono acting out various characters and his onstage persona.[11] Like Bob Dylan, Bono sang about the evils of war and consumerism, while each band member wore outrageous and flashy costumes.

"Out Of Control," a number that Bono wrote on his eighteenth birthday, is U2's first single from 1978. The first time a U2 performance appeared in the news was March 20, 1978. The *Evening Press* in Ireland reported on four "Dublin schoolboys [who] carried off the top prize at the Limerick Civic Week Pop '78 Competition. . . . Bono expressed that U2's success will 'solve our money problems in a big way, particularly in regard to equipment. Now we hope to be able to buy a van.'"[12]

In 1979, the four borrowed money from family and friends to seek press support and a record deal. A few months later, a three-track record, titled *Three*, was recorded and went straight onto Ireland's music charts. In December of that year, U2 traveled to London for their first shows outside of their home country. Not unlike the Beatles, the British press took note of U2's genuine sounds right away, claiming that the Irishmen took England by storm.

Not being British or American, U2 comes from a different tradition than most pop stars. In Ireland, the band had all the room they needed to experiment and find their own sounds. "It's a very important part of the way we work, this insular type of development we've had where we haven't been exposed in the first nine months to a trendy, cliquey atmosphere that you have in London," Bono once explained.[13]

For years, U2 knew they had something special. By the beginning of 1980, U2 won five categories in the Readers' Poll of *Hot Press*. The band held out for a decent recording contract, despite the offers that flooded in. The same year, U2 signed with Island Records and prepared to conquer America. Not as monumental as the Beatles on *Sullivan*, U2's US debut in December of 1980 was at the Ritz in New York City.

In an article in *Melody Maker* later that year, Bono described U2 as "four people, four individuals, four friends." Meanwhile, the journalist discussed the lead singer's bizarre "dress, his motions, his imaginative use of language, and almost fervent desire to be heard and understood."[14]

In 1980, U2 entered a studio for the first time with their new label, Island Records, and recorded their debut album, *Boy*. According to Adam, the well-rounded record has picturesque lyrics and is an ideal representation of U2's adolescence. The themes of the band's echo-drenched singles were innocence, adolescence, and growth; *Boy* has a child's face on its cover.

Critics immediately recognized the passion of U2's music. Their fame grew right away, with the selling of tens of millions of albums; they have held the top position in almost every chart around the globe. Of course, U2 benefited enormously from MTV and its publicity. The band's visual sense, along with Bono's presence on the small screen, made U2 a favorite on the cable network. The band proved to be crucially "videogenic at a time when MTV had more influence on teens and pop culture than radio and print combined."[15]

In Europe, U2 built a minuscule following with their live shows. It was time for them to sell their sound to the largest record market in the world, America. A miniature tour began in New York on December 6, 1980, usually with no more than two hundred spectators at each gig. But on December 8, 1980, John Lennon was assassinated. The horrifying news inspired U2's raging performance that next night in Toronto. The band went on to play over two hundred shows in 1981.

"We're not a 'new wave' band. We're not a punk band. I don't know what the hell we are, we are just U2. We're individual," Bono announced in April of 1981 on University of Chicago's WNVR radio. A few months later, Tim Sommer of *Trouser Press* reported that the band's "sweeping and majestic music is 'rock' in one sense, but simultaneously transcends all genres," in the way that much of the Beatles' sounds were hard to categorize.[16]

U2's second record was released in 1981, entitled *October* for the time of the album's release, as well as the autumnal nature of its material. Not breaking into the US Top 100, *October* hit number eleven on the British charts, proving that U2 was not a one-hit-wonder. It consisted of a new theme for U2: coping with manhood. The introspective record was dramatic and showed the band's motorization.

U2 toured the states for a second time, now as the opening act for the J. Geils Band. The road trip concluded after sixty shows in three months. Halfway through the tour, Bono and the Edge were interviewed on WBCN radio in New Haven, Connecticut. "It's very important for us to tour, because, you know, a lot of bands put out records and then sit back and wait for it to happen," explained Bono. "We want to play to people face to face and let them make up their own minds." In New York City, the band received their first standing ovation in March 1982.[17]

The four musicians decided to get political with their 1983 record *War*. Bono's lyrics openly expressed opposition to violence of all types. "New Year's Day" was U2's first commercial success, not unlike the Beatles "Love Me Do" in 1964. It is the one single on *War* that reached the UK's Top 10, as well U2's first song in America's Top 100 chart, eventually peaking at number fifty-three.

According to *Into the Heart*, a U2 book of lyrics, "New Year's Day" is a love song written for the singer's wife, with an "impressionistic political backdrop."[18] It is representative of the Solidarity movement for justice against Poland's then-communist regime.

"Revolution" was the Beatles' first overt political statement. The song was written about Vietnam and a much-needed revolution in the third-world country. John believed that the only worthwhile revolution would come about with individual inner change, opposed to revolutionary violence.

Similarly, "Sunday Bloody Sunday" is a number about twelve double agents that were killed in 1972. The fourteen civilians were shot dead when the Paratroop Regiment of the British Army took charge of a civil rights demonstration in the Irish city of Derry. The number's "violent imagery" directly challenges Northern Ireland's political unrest. Bono introduces "Sunday Bloody Sunday" by explaining, "This is not a rebel song," and begins singing, "I can't believe the news today."[19]

"This was where we started to find our agenda. . . . [*War* is a] record about being taken seriously," explained Adam in 2001. "'Sunday Bloody Sunday' was a song we needed to do. . . . We felt that was a valid subject, as opposed to happy, shiny pop music."[20]

Bono has always wanted to make political statements. "People have to speak out," Bono said in 1983. "Things have to be done. We can't all lie down. But at the same time, I don't put on a '60s uniform."[21] U2's American *War* tour was a campaign against the everyday radio format. The biggest reason for the album's success was because of new fans gained on the road in small stadiums and college auditoriums. In fact, the tour's slogan was "U2 Declare War on Boring Music."[22]

Along the same lines, the Beatles' manager Brian Epstein once complained that no radio stations would play a seven-minute single. John simply responded, "They will if it's us," and "Hey Jude" is the Fab Four's most successful single, spending an astonishing nine weeks at number one, and nineteen in the Top 40 of the American chart in 1968.[23] The single raked in $5 million in 1968 alone, and over $7.5 million by 1972. *Billboard* ranked "Hey Jude" in second place on the magazine's biggest hits of the past two decades chart in 1976.[24]

Bono's climbing on the stage in June of 1983 made for disastrous results. Waving a white flag while moving to a balcony during "Electric Co.," he risked his own safety and either jumped or fell into the crowd twenty feet below. Of course, hundreds of fans rushed to touch Bono, tearing his clothes into pieces, until his tour manager led him to safety. Later Bono told *Rolling Stone*, "I lost my senses completely. . . . Somebody could have died at that concert; it was a real sickener for me. It's meant a total reevaluation of what we are about live. We don't need to use a battering ram. It has to be down to the music."[25]

The *U2 Live at Red Rocks* video sold well, introducing the onstage excitement of their concerts to a global audience. Fully supported by FM radio as well, U2 built an audience after years on the road in both Europe and the States by the early '80s. When the band traveled to Australia, they began selling out arenas right away. "If we stay in clubs," Bono said earnestly in 1983, "we'll develop small minds, and we'll start making small music."[26]

Utilizing the audience interaction, as well as the scenic landscape, U2's *Under a Blood Red Sky* was recorded live in Colorado the same year. This was the band's most religious stage of their careers. The lyric "Under a blood red sky," from the song "New Year's Day," refers to the "moon to blood" prophecy from the biblical book of Joel. Also, "A crowd has gathered in black and white" is a reference to gathering people of all races, creeds, and colors. For the first week of its release, the album topped British charts. However, *Under a Blood Red Sky* experienced a gradual acceleration into the Top 10 in the arms of America.

The 1984 record *The Unforgettable Fire* was named after paintings by survivors of the Hiroshima and Nagasaki bombings. "We wanted to get into something atmospheric and textual," explained the Edge. "The music has such a strong voice, that Bono's vocals are almost like another musical element."[27]

In the 1980s, U2 was appearing on the cover of music magazines, such as *Rock Scene*, *Concert Shots*, and *Teen*. The band's trademark was the Edge's massive depth of field, containing a continual rhythm. Also, Bono had two discrete singing voices, one for muttering verses, and another for high-pitched choruses.

The Unforgettable Fire contains a song written about Martin Luther King Jr. When Bono began penning "Pride (In the Name of Love)," he was planning on an ode to Ronald Reagan. But when U2 visited the Chicago Peace Museum, the singer was immediately inspired by the civil rights leader who had been shot in 1968. Bono changed the number's emphasis to rouse black people. "Pride" became the first single on *The Unforgettable Fire* and an American Top 40 radio hit in 1984.

In interviews, Bono explained he used lyrics on the "visual" album to allow listeners to form their own meanings from his words. For example, the U2 numbers "Wire" and "Bad" concentrate on drug addiction and its fatal effects. Yet Bono's verses were written with enough imagery to allow listeners to draw their own interpretations.

In 1984, U2 performed in both Band Aid and Farm Aid, trying to help those in need. Band Aid spurred Bono's personal concern for famine in Africa. On July 13, 1985, the largest ever TV audience for a live music event formed for Live Aid, and U2 stole the show. The rock star was later enlightened again when he and his wife traveled to Ethiopia and spent six weeks working with children in an orphanage. The experience remained with him into Jubilee. The year after Live Aid, U2 headlined the "Conspiracy of Hope" tour. The concerts performed for Amnesty International's twenty-fifth anniversary included legendary names, such as Lou Reed, Peter Gabriel, and the Police.

U2 was selling out stadiums throughout 1985. Due to their endless globetrotting, *The Unforgettable Fire* reached number twelve in the States and turned gold three months after its release. Eventually, the record sold one million copies, giving U2 their first platinum album. The American public's reaction on the Unforgettable Fire Tour is not unlike the Beatles' first quest through the States in 1964. U2 fan behavior, as well as the four boys' safety, became an issue for the first time, as fanatics would go crazy over the musicians. Just like the Beatles, the simple presence of Bono, the Edge, Adam, or Larry would send thousands of fans screaming in hysterics, jumping on cars, desperate to touch a member of the rock-and-roll band.

In 1987, *The Joshua Tree* became the fastest-selling recording of all time in the United States, and still remains U2's top moneymaker. The band's fifth studio album started at number seven on US charts and flew to number one in both the United States and the United Kingdom at the same time, eventually selling more than fourteen million copies. U2 toured in front of three million

The Edge, 2001, *photo by Sean McCloskey*

spectators and grossed more than $40 million in '87 alone. "That was our first taste of success on that scale, and the ground moved a bit," said Clayton.[28]

U2 was now considered the biggest rock act of the decade. *The Joshua Tree* was emotional and heartfelt. The four Irishmen's music was fun to dance to, while filled with societies' history and current morals. As journalist Pimm Jal De La Parra explained, the album's songs contain a "belief in the human spirit, and its ability to survive amid personal, political and economic setbacks." Adam and Larry's sounds were reported as rhythmic, while "Bono and the Edge add layers of chiming guitar and soaring vocals."[29]

Bono once expressed that "Where the Streets Have No Name" was U2's best-written song to that time. The cut is a modern-day version of a journey into the unknown, as well as a world free of religious and racial divide, with its roots in gospel. *Imagine* all the people who could have influenced the images correlated on "Where the Streets Have No Name."[30] The pop single "I Still Haven't Found What I'm Looking For" went to number one in the States. The message of the entire record is doubt and faith. The message has been a U2 theme since day one.

Strongly supported by MTV, *The Joshua Tree*'s "With or Without You" rose to *Billboard*'s number one on the American singles charts, where it stayed for three weeks. The ballad is about one anxious man's doubt and guilt coinciding in a grim relationship. "Bullet the Blue Sky," another memorable tune off of *The Joshua Tree,* is about the greed and corruption in America, and its foreign policy, during the Ronald Reagan era. The members of U2 felt that the president was being hypocritical, closed-minded, and unfair when it came to relations with foreign powers. Bono expresses no contempt in his political number "Bullet the Blue Sky."

Bono reflects on the 1980s shadow of heroin in Dublin with the ballad "Running to Stand Still." After all, illegal drugs have been synonymous with rock and roll for decades. Yet the subject was rarely addressed in popular music thirty-five years ago during the Beatles' reign. When John Lennon was determined to conceive a healthy child with Yoko in August of 1969, he quit using heroin as an artistic indulgence. He wrote a song about the process. "Cold Turkey" is John's personal document of the painful process of breaking the addiction by abrupt abstinence. Two physical symptoms of stopping heroin use are clammy skin and goose bumps; hence the song title. When the other Beatles rejected the song, John was forced to record "Cold Turkey" as a solo project later that year.

Toward the end of 1987, United Press International named Bono one of "America's 10 Sexiest Men," along with Tom Cruise and Michael Jordan.[31] Bono expressed that *The Joshua Tree* was U2's best work. At the same time, he promised, "It will not be our best record by a long shot."[32]

The year 1988 brought *Rattle and Hum*, along with U2's Lovetown Tour. The album about U2's "return to simplicity"

Adam Clayton, *photo by Sean McCloskey*

captures what the band was experiencing on the second half of the Joshua Tree tour. The phenomenal trek lasted 264 days in fifteen different counties. U2 performed over one hundred shows in seventy-two venues, for over three million fans in one year. The Irish band invited a forty-member film crew on the second leg of the Joshua Tree tour in America, and *Rattle and Hum* became a big Hollywood affair. The movie benefited from considerable promotion and publicity, turning many U2 fans off. It ceases to be a documentary, as *Rattle and Hum* offers no new information to U2 followers.

Rattle and Hum opens with a line about the infamous murderer Charles Manson and a cover of the Beatles' "Helter Skelter," recorded at Denver's McNichols Arena in November of 1987. "Desire" is about the contradictions of being a successful rock star. The song may remind listeners of Lennon's hypocritical teachings of feeding the poor, while he once maintained a private room while visiting a New York City hospital, solely for his fur coats. Tracing rock's American roots, U2 toured Elvis' home at Graceland, as well as church gospels in Harlem, for *Rattle and Hum*. They performed the bluesy single "When Love Comes to Town" with American legend B. B. King. Along with "God Part II," U2 also covers Bob Dylan's "All Along the Watchtower," with Bono adding the line, "All I've got is a red guitar, three chords and the truth."

The final song on *Rattle and Hum*, "All I Want Is You," is a number about commitment. "I'm interested in the idea of marriage. I think it's madness, but it's a grand madness," said Bono. "I think that's why a lot of people fall apart, because they're not prepared for what it is."[33]

"U2 are without doubt the biggest band in the world," reported *Spin* in 1989. Binding sex and spirituality, the fastest-selling record in British history went double platinum in England on advance sales alone. Just like Bono about two years prior, the Edge told Ted Mico of *Spin* magazine that U2 had not written their best material yet. *Achtung Baby* was soon to come.[34]

The Beatles' *Sgt. Pepper's Lonely Hearts Club Band* is considered by many critics as the greatest album ever recorded. The stereo album *Sgt. Pepper's* was purposely recorded too technical to hit the road with, as the pandemonium associated with the Beatles' concerts, such as the crowd's screams overpowering the music, was too much for the boys to handle. Similarly, Elvis and Dylan gave up touring for a period after hitting the top and devoted themselves to making records and living with their wives and children. On the other hand, U2's 1991 Zoo TV Tour, almost twenty-five years later, was the "biggest, loudest, most expensive and technically ambitious rock tour in history."[35]

"Pop music is what's happening," Bono explained in 2001. "There's a visceral side to that music, which is something you could call rock. It's that physical thing that Jimi Hendrix and Led Zeppelin did. . . . It's powerful."[36]

Achtung Baby was recorded in Berlin, over the metropolis of skyscrapers during the cold winter of 1990. The environment, a "surreal junkyard" as Bono referred to it, "tapped into the seismic social, political and musical shifts that were shaking the world at the end of the Thatcher-Reagan era." *Achtung Baby* "was a deliberate attempt to step out of the mainstream, to challenge audiences and to confound critics."[37]

Achtung Baby's themes of faith and faithlessness suggest what pop star Elvis Costello called "emotional fascism" and the dictatorship of fidelity. The record's timeless hits on both the radio and MTV include "The Fly," "Mysterious Ways," "One," and "Until the End of the World." "Underneath that thin layer of trash it's blood and guts. It's a very heavy, loaded record. It's a dense record," Bono declared with a devilish grin.[38]

The Zoo TV tour lasted almost two years as "a multimedia extravaganza that set a new level for stadium-level productions." The stage was covered with giant logos for fast-food joints, not unlike the billboards on a crowded highway. Artist Willie Williams drew sketches for a stage design splattered with the logos of Burger King, Shell, Sony, Heinz, Singer, Betty Crocker, Fruit of the Loom, and a dozen other corporations, with three house-size TVs in the middle. Similarly to Elvis, Bono dyed his brown hair black and sported a black leather suit, turning himself into the personification of a rockin' cat.[39]

Inspired by *Achtung Baby*'s world tour, U2 was flying so high on Zoo TV, the band did not want to come down. U2 decided to take the energy into the studio and record the emotional *Zooropa* in 1993. Backed by the single "Lemon," sung by the Edge, the shows displayed even more enormous screens with off-the-wall imagery than Zoo TV. For example, the concerts showed Nazi videos and a "Zoo TV Confessional," featuring fifteen seconds of audience members spilling their guts to the crowd. Bono wore heavy makeup, sporting the Fly sunglasses and devil's horns to create the ultimate egomaniac, "Bono Macphisto." Along with regular parodies of Bono on *Saturday Night Live*, there were countless requests seeking Bono as the lead villain in the Hollywood

Bono, *photo by Sean McCloskey*

film *Johnny Mnemonic*, as well as an offer to create a "Macphisto" character for *Batman Forever*.

Even more disappointing to fans than *Zooropa* may have been the album *Pop*, released in 1997. Fusing dance, electronica, and the club world, *Pop* is considered the first and only dud in U2's extensive career. George Harrison and the Beatles' influence snuck into the record with the line "and the sun, sun, here it comes" in the single "Last Night on Earth." Yet, Bono's lyrics lack poetry, and the album failed to contain a Top 10 hit on either side of the Atlantic. Similar to those of *Zooropa*, the profits from *Pop* were unsatisfactory by U2's multiplatinum standards. The corresponding PopMart tour, filled with even more extensive technology and hoopla, failed to sell out stadiums. U2 should have focused on more radio-friendly songs to sell to the mass public.

"I thought we had a record of quite extraordinary music, but I accept that a lot of people didn't get it," said Adam. "What can I say? We made a mistake. But it was a grand mistake!"[40] Bono once defended pop music to *Time* magazine by claiming, "It's forgotten the discipline of the 45 and the shock therapy that Nirvana brought to the pop charts that the Sex Pistols had and the Stones and the Beatles. We're in a new era of progressive rock."[41]

U2 made it back to the top in the new millennium by "returning to the basics" in 2000.[42] The band's tenth studio album, *All that You Can't Leave Behind*, featured the Grammy-winning single "Beautiful Day." U2's world tour, which kicked off in Sunrise, Florida, made them the top-grossing act of 2001. The concerts actually "became cultural touchstones following [the deadly assaults on] September 11."[43] U2 performed in Madison Square Garden a few weeks after the attacks. Of course, Bono's sermon on world peace did not leave a dry eye in New York's arena.

In November of 2004, U2 released their eleventh studio album, *How to Dismantle an Atomic Bomb*. Right away, the media proclaimed the album to be a masterpiece. Winning Album of the Year at the forty-eighth annual Grammy Awards, some magazines even went so far as to call *How to Dismantle* the band's greatest work. An arrogant Bono boasts about the record by claiming U2 successfully weaves sex, religion, and politics together.

Since the new millennium, Bono has been effectively using his global fame to benefit those less fortunate. Associations on the rock star's resume now include Amnesty International for human rights, Greenpeace, Freedom for the Southeast Asian Nations and a chair beside Bill Gates as a cofounder of the African activist group DATA (debt, AIDS, trade, Africa). He was nominated for a Nobel Peace Prize and even met the pope; he and producer Quincy Jones poked fun at the holy man's "pimp shoes." According to veteran journalist David Fricke of *Rolling Stone*, Bono was born for politics, as "his lobbying techniques come naturally."[44] Adam later explained to the United Kingdom's *Q* magazine that his fearless leader is a "grown-up" who definitely "knows his business."[45]

Few other pop bands today have remained successful in the industry for as long as Bono and U2. Such notable acts include Georgia's R.E.M., whose sound has remained in the same progressive genre for decades, and the ever-changing Beastie Boys. Meanwhile, U2 has spent the last quarter century paving the way into the American spotlight for other Irish acts, such as Sinead O'Conner, Enya, and the Cranberries.

One reason for U2's prolonged success is the natural bond between the four friends who grew up together in Dublin. They each criticize one another's work, helping U2's music to stay relevant in the world's mainstream. They are best mates and have an integral role in one another's lives. U2 insists that all songs appearing on their albums are credited to the band, as opposed to Lennon and McCartney battling over royalties. U2 has remained on top, experiencing zero member changes and no temporary breakups.

"People think the band is this unit that's always together," explained Larry in the book *U2 at the End of the World*. "There is a love between the members of this band that is deeper than whatever comes between us."[46] Sure, the four boys still disagree about song titles, their order, and so forth. Yet each member of U2 has treated the others with respect and generosity. In 1989, Bono told Ted Mico of *Spin*, "We'll keep releasing record after record until everyone'll be sick of us."[47]

4

"God" vs. "God Part II"

SPIRITUAL POETRY

THE SONG "GOD" is John Lennon's explicit exposition of his outlook of the world in 1970, just two months before the Beatles officially broke up. The highly personal song was an attempt for John to counsel all Beatles fans to accept his work as a solo artist, and it is quite memorable. In the fall of 2004, Yoko released a new LP of Lennon material, but the *Acoustic* version of "God" is a drop in sound recording quality compared to the *Anthology* edition.

John offers a list of concepts and false idols in which he no longer believes. "I don't believe in Beatles" is perhaps the most notable verse. The accidental distortion that kicks in on the bass during his powerful, repetitive "I don't believe" sequence may remind listeners of Neil Young's haunting "Dead Man." On the *Acoustic* release, John replaces "I don't believe in Zimmerman" with the less cryptic "I don't believe in Dylan." The song continues with his cold statement of faith in himself, "I just believe in me," and sums up with, "The dream is over."

Bono, for his part, is a fantastic, sophisticated writer. He wrote "God Part II," recorded on 1988's *Rattle and Hum*, as a direct response to Lennon's "God." Of course, "Part II" is far more deliberately poetic, using symbolism, quoting modern journalists, and with Bono mocking himself. Bono's lyrics are more general than Lennon's, allowing listeners to draw their own representations from private experiences. Lennon dives right into deep water when he kicks off his version by disclaiming his love for God and His book. Right away, the listener feels the distance between the rock star and the church. Bono makes a reference to Lennon seeking "the truth." *Gimme Some Truth: The John Lennon FBI Files* is Jon Wiener's 2000 book about the superstar's possible risk to national security.

Bono claims, "Success is to give." Activists around the world know this to be the case following Bono's direct involvement with charitable organizations such as Live Aid. Starting with the Toronto Peace Festival in 1969, John, with Yoko, did a series of rock concerts as their statement of Peace and Love, and to spotlight various social issues effectively. All proceeds from the concerts were given to the needy. In the summer of 1972, John Lennon performed at a charity concert in Madison Square Garden as well. The show was successful in improving the living conditions for mentally handicapped children around the globe.

Bono mocks himself when he sings, "Don't believe in riches, but you should see where I live." The man owns quite exquisite homes around the world, including in Dublin, New York City, Miami, and next door to Elton John in the south of France. Listeners may be immediately reminded of Lennon's charitable acts. On *John and Yoko's Year of Peace*, a documentary from 1969, the Beatle catches a homeless drifter sleeping in his backyard. John invites the gentleman in and cooks him breakfast. Would Lennon have performed such an act if a video camera were not present? Would Bono be any different?

Again, Bono relates his song to Lennon when he sings, "I believe in love." In John's "God," the poet claims, "I just believe in me. Yoko and me." Bono's devilish alter ego, along with its hidden desires, brilliantly appears when he claims not to believe in "forced

Oil painting of John Lennon, *by Todd McFliker*

entry," "But every time she passes by, wild thoughts escape." There's
a reference to peace when he disregards an "Uzi" for his belief in
mere love. The Irish singer does not "believe in cocaine." Similarly,
as noted, Lennon discusses his overcoming of heroin in the number
"Cold Turkey." Bono sings he already has "a speedball" in his head.
It may not be hard for listeners to understand why he would have a
natural high after the nightly experience of a stadium's worth of
fans singing his poetry word for word. The optimist in Bono comes
out when he sings, "Don't believe them when they tell me there
ain't no cure." In 2004 alone, the man earned $5 million for AIDS
research in Africa. The rock star met with George W. Bush in
the White House, yet never removed his sunglasses.

U2's lead singer does not believe in Goldman. Albert Goldman was an infamous reporter who wrote accusing and heartbreaking versions of both Elvis' and Lennon's biographies. Bono uses a double entendre when he sings, "His type [is] like a curse," and pulls from the Lennon catalog, singing, "Instant karma's gonna get him." He refers to the Beatles changing the world with rock and roll. The poet uses a double entendre a second time when he sings about the world spinning "in revolution," referring to the earth's orbital rotation, as well as the Fab Four's overthrowing effects on society. Bono's dream is not over, as his career as a pop star spirals and turns after a quarter century of living the life. "God Part II" discusses a singer on the radio. The voice says he will "kick the darkness, till it bleeds daylight." The phrase is a quote from Elvis protégé and legendary songwriter Bruce Cockburn.

Bono claims to be spinning on a wheel, as opposed to John, who merely sat back to watch the "wheels go round and round." Rather than avoiding the public eye, Bono embraces the attention. A veteran in show business, he presently collects Grammys, makes millions in record sales, and sells out stadiums worldwide. The dream is not over for Bono, as he is still feeling the spotlight's presence and walking tall. After all, Bono firmly believes that all you need is love to solve the world's most prevalent tribulations.

5

Records of a Generation

SGT. PEPPER'S VS. ACHTUNG BABY

SPREADING TO THE MASSES, the Beatles' *Sgt. Pepper's Lonely Hearts Club Band* is ranked number one GREATEST ALBUM OF ALL TIME in the December 2003 issue of *Rolling Stone*.[1] The timeless LP richly defines the transitional 1960s, as the Beatles rewrote the rules for recording popular music. Paul came up with the fictional Lonely Hearts Club Band, an Edwardian brass four-some. Transporting the four musicians' roles to the psychedelic 1960s allowed the Beatles more freedom to experiment. The album shaped the notion of the musician as a true artist. The release of *Sgt Pepper's* took baby boomers for a wild ride, as it was society's first taste of "acid rock." Engineered not to be performed live, *Sgt. Pepper's* stands as "the most important album ever made, an unsurpassed adventure," something that popular culture has ever experienced.[2] Relaying messages of love and risqué poetry to the youth culture, the Beatles revolutionized media with the production of *Sgt. Pepper's*, while U2 changed the channel with *Achtung Baby* and its industrial world tour, Zoo TV.

U2's *Achtung Baby* and its Zoo TV world tour were successfully constructed as the "biggest, loudest, most expensive, and technically ambitious" concert production in history, staged in front of three million spectators worldwide in 1992 and 1993.[3] It is not a stretch to say that *Achtung Baby* is the *Sgt. Pepper's* of the MTV Generation. The 1991 album marked the first and greatest of the postmodern movement, flaunting cultural values by concocting an album, as well as a world tour, marked by nonsense. Ranked number sixty-two in *Rolling Stone*'s "Greatest Albums of All Time" in 2002, *Achtung Baby* is the finest representation of the time period's media-excessive culture, exaggerated with sardonic humor.[4]

Proving the Beatles' popularity is a result of true talent, rather than mere performers in bowl-cuts and matching suits, *Sgt. Pepper's* is the best work in the band's eight-year history together. The record was released during the Summer of Love, San Francisco's hippie movement in June of 1967. Winning four Grammys, including Best Album, *Sgt. Pepper's* defines the Beatles and their timeless legacy. *Achtung Baby* was nominated for 1992's Album of the Year but eventually lost to Eric Clapton's *Unplugged*. U2 turned down an offer to play at the award ceremony before the envelope was opened.

The creation of *Sgt. Pepper's* was an achievement unlike any previous in mass media's history. The Beatles began distorting their vocals and guitars three days after experiencing Jimi Hendrix blow the roof off of London's Saville Theatre in January 1967. *Sgt. Pepper's* was conceived only to be created in a studio, as live performances were too chaotic for the Beatles to actually perform. "We decided to go into another art form," explained the band's producer, George Martin. "We are devising something that couldn't be done any other way."[5] Each member of the band devoted hundreds of hours to studio time, taking five months to complete the record.

Whereas *Sgt. Pepper's* was conceived with no intention of being performed live, Zoo TV was staged as the largest rock concert in touring history. From 1980 to 1987, U2 toured the States nonstop with spiritual and minimalist performances. But for the next four years, U2 took it's time recuperating after *Rattle and Hum*'s Love-town tour. Zoo TV sold out every show, thirty-two arenas, within the year. From the get-go, critics recognized U2's introspective material and claimed *Achtung Baby* as a classic. The industrial dance rhythms were a new twist for the band. U2 played for thousands of screaming fans each night while "maintaining a direct, personal, almost confessional relationship with the audience."[6] *Achtung Baby* was the number one record worldwide, selling more than seven million copies around the globe before U2 even began its two-year road trip.

In the early 1990s, Bono became interested in the zoo as a metaphor. The concert included a technical staff of two hundred, a stage's worth of electronic paraphernalia, and an intimate podium for the second set of the 1980s classics. In the tradition of Led Zeppelin, U2 flew on its own private jet, Zoo Airlines, and each of the band members earned 1–2 percent of the show's phenomenal profits.

The Zoo TV extravaganza mirrored the absurdity in the culture's overemphasized mass media. Spectators were amused by the futuristic set design by artist William Gibson, featuring hollow cars painted in fluorescent colors. U2's stage represented East Berlin with the bright lights of the Vegas strip. Reporter Stephen Dalton cleverly described Zoo TV as an "orgy of superstar excess and multimedia overload."[7] Perhaps it is more than a coincidence that U2's opening act was the Disposable Heroes of Hypocrisy, whose signature tune is "Television, Drug of the Nation."

News bulletins, funny scenes, and embarrassing messages from the crowd were flaunted on Zoo TV's thirty-six color monitors and video walls. One of them displayed an ongoing sequence of words on the screen: "Luxury," "Chaos," "Condom," "Flower." Eventually full phrases would appear: "Everything You Know Is Wrong," "I'd Like to Teach the World to Sing," and "It's Your World—You Can Change It." Wrapped in the Fly sunglasses and lizard-skin pants, Bono would frequently phone a politician and a local pizza joint from the Zoo's stage. Guest appearances were made by Public Enemy and Lou Reed, who duetted with

American tourists crossing Abbey Road in 1996

Bono on "Satellite of Love." Midway through the colossal tour, the four members of U2 formed the message "H-E-L-P," parodying the Beatles on the cover of their 1965 *Help!* LP. This event occurred, in front of press cameras, on the shoreline of Colombia after the quartet had symbolically dumped sand from an Irish beach there.

According to George Harrison, the comfort level while making *Sgt Pepper's* in Abbey Road Studios could have been improved. In the heart of London, the Beatles worked in an enormous white room that desperately needed to be swept and painted. "It was all dirty," George described. "It wasn't a very nice atmosphere." Despite the studio's lack of cleanliness, the four musicians grabbed "hold of the faders and the mixers" to take part in "the revolution of making recordings."[8] Today the studio still stands in London. There are no tours offered to the public, but a visiting musician may scale the crosswalk and play a guitar on the steps of Abbey Road, paying tribute to the four.

Despite the bedlam of Berlin's dark streets, *Achtung Baby* "shines even brighter amidst the trash and junk," according to Bono. In 1991, he explained to *Uncut* that *Achtung Baby* is U2's best work to date. "There is a lot of blood and guts on that record . . . there is a lot of soul."[9]

Zoo Berlin poster

Overlooking the metropolis of skyscrapers during the cold winter of 1990, U2's *Achtung Baby* was created in Berlin. Three years after *Rattle and Hum* was released, the band's seventh studio album was extremely tedious to assemble. U2 utilized Hansa-by-the-Wall studios, where David Bowie recorded "Heroes" in 1977. The environment, a "surreal junkyard" as Bono referred to it, "tapped into the seismic social, political, and musical shifts that were shaking the world at the end of the Thatcher-Reagan Era."[10] Within the year following *Achtung Baby*'s release, Seattle grunge music appeared with Nirvana's mainstream breakthrough, the Soviet Union collapsed, Nelson Mandela was released from prison, the World Wide Web debuted in Switzerland, and the first American Gulf War commenced and was concluded.

In *U2: Into the Heart*, Niall Stokes vividly recreates the ambiance of *Achtung Baby*'s sessions. The author details the European businessmen swarming the streets of Berlin, along with prostitutes, "pimps, pick-pockets and transients."[11] "It was a gold rush in full swing, without the gold," he wrote.[12] The city's mayhem portrayed a turning point for the fall of communism in Europe.

U2's revolutionary release borrowed its title from West Berlin's main transport hub. *Achtung Baby* explored uncharted territory of hip-hop beats, drum machines, house rhythms, distorted vocals, and a hard industrial edge. Bono once described "Zoo Station," the first song on *Achtung Baby*, as "the sound of four men chopping down *The Joshua Tree*." *Achtung Baby* is ranked number twenty-six in *Rolling Stone's* "Greatest Albums of All Time."[13] The techno record expresses U2's playful statement of intent, "to embark on a journey into the unknown."[14]

The Beatles and U2 are two of only a handful of bands that could afford the expensive studio time to try new ideas with their material. At the same time, the general public would not even pay attention to these new sounds had the bands not already possessed a proven track record. By the middle of their careers, both the Fab Four and the Irish quartet could experiment musically, as sales were not necessarily a primary concern. The two ensembles had the luxury to dictate anything they wanted to record, as was the case with *Sgt. Pepper's* and *Achtung Baby*.

With this newfound freedom in the studio, Paul conceived *Sgt. Pepper's*. The *Lonely Hearts Club Band* allowed the four to escape their impossible expectations as Beatles. "I had this song written of Sgt. Pepper, who, twenty years ago today, taught us to play and we're his protégés and here we are," he said.[15] According to journalist Steve Turner, *Sgt. Pepper's* was the Beatles' freedom to explore new avenues, "writing old-fashioned lyrics delivered with a satirical psychedelic intensity."[16]

"I'm sad, because Britain is going the American way in this," Paul explained when asked about the technical costs spent on *Sgt. Pepper's* studio time. "I know we four would be scruffy, dirty and obscene to the Americans if we didn't have money."[17] Bono once told *Rolling Stone*, "We have a responsibility to abuse our position. Because we had been spoiled financially, we had what Groucho Marx called 'fuck-off money.' If you waste that, you're a wanker, you don't deserve anything."[18]

Not unlike the band members from *Sgt. Pepper's Lonely Hearts Club Band*, the Fly was created by U2's fearless leader. Bono's new alter-ego image allowed the artist to mock his role as a media giant. "When I put on these glasses, anything gives," Bono once explained to a reporter. "I've learned to be insincere and I've learned to lie. I've never felt better."[19] The distortion in the Fly's voice gave listeners enough distance from the classic U2 material of the 1980s. The new persona helped make *Achtung Baby* the band's freshest work yet.

In 2003, no less an authority than Elvis Costello claimed that *Sgt. Pepper's* has directly influenced every English-speaking culture, from Motown and Nashville to Europe and Australia. Created in Abbey Road's Studio Two in January of 1967, *Sgt. Pepper's* "encouraged the belief that limits to the imagination were culturally imposed and should therefore be challenged," said journalist Steve Turner.[20]

The worldwide success of *Sgt. Pepper's* influenced "acid rock." Along with the hippie culture's hallucinogenic drugs, an antiestablishment counterculture developed, particularly strong among antiwar, peace-loving hippies in Northern California. Psychedelic bands emerged on both sides of the Atlantic, experimenting with improvised jams. English bands, such as the fearless Pink Floyd, as well as American musicians, such as the Grateful Dead, responded to *Sgt. Pepper's* by pursuing overlapping technologies. Linking two unfinished songs to create the masterpiece "A Day in the Life," the multitracking techniques used by the Beatles forever altered the way pop music is recorded.

In the early '90s, *Achtung Baby's* technical recording indicated U2's quest for developing a revitalized sound, consisting of a "postindustrial buzz," with experimental vocals. Meanwhile, the band's Zoo TV global trek inspired the next decade's worth of massive world tours. Followers of Bono's engineered singing voice include the American band Live as well as the British Coldplay. In the spirit of Zoo TV, a group of surfers out of Los Angeles known as Jane's Addiction performed a global stint full of an array of eye candy in 2001. Lustful dancers and juggling gymnasts graced the stage's strip-club atmosphere. It was a visual feast of Christmas lights, lasers, and dancers arranged onstage, with a hand-painted backdrop of white and black bricks.

"Sgt. Pepper's Lonely Hearts Club Band" is the first song on the Beatles' timeless release. The number introduces the boys as new characters from the past with no prior expectations to live up to. "Zoo Station," *Achtung Baby's* introduction, tells listeners that U2 is "ready for what's next." Bono is "Ready to let go of the steering wheel" and travel backward in time as well: "Time is a train /

Makes the future the past / Leaves you standing in the station / With your face pressed up against the glass."

Along with middle-class family values and home improvement, the underlying theme of the Beatles record is simple love. U2's dozen songs all focus on the hardships associated with a disorderly relationship. Obvious to listeners, the songs on *Achtung Baby* were all written from a frustrated and heartbroken man's point of view.

"With a Little Help from My Friends" is the Beatles' childlike sing-along about honest companionships. The entire song's simple lyrics, such as "I just need someone to love. / I want somebody to love," were completed in the studio, where ten takes were recorded in one long evening. *Achtung Baby's* "The Fly" claims, "It's no secret that a friend is someone who lets you help." The first single off of the album is "a bracing, exciting change of pace for U2 that heralds a new chapter for the still very important band." Bono told David Fricke of *Rolling Stone* that "The Fly" was "written like a phone call from hell, but the guy liked it there."[21]

Sgt. Pepper's contains "Getting Better," a very optimistic number about love. When asked about the song, John admitted that "Getting Better" refers to his aggression associated with everyday peace and love. "I used to be cruel to my woman, I beat her and kept her apart from the things that she loved," he sings.

Bono becomes a pessimistic poet in the masochistic "So Cruel." Written about the collapse of the Edge's seven-year marriage to Aislinn O'Sullivan, "So Cruel" is a man's dismal grievance about being burnt in the game of love: "You put your lips to her lips to stop the lie." Yet the heartbroken and desperate husband remains infatuated with his tormentor, even after he was betrayed by infidelity. When a reporter asked the musicians to name the themes of the U2 LP, the Edge claimed: "betrayal, love, morality, spirituality, and faith. Love is evil on *Achtung Baby*."[22]

"Mysterious Ways" is a fast-beat serenade concerning women in general giving little or no romance whatsoever to their men. "It's about everything that goes with the breakdown of one relationship and starting up another," Bono explained.[23] Similarly,

"Acrobat" is based on deceit and its effects on relationships. The man in the song's feelings of desperation reflect the emotional climate that remains consistent throughout the entire album.

While recording "Within You Without You," George was the only Beatle present in the studio, along with session musicians who played violin, cello, and other instruments. Mr. Harrison first became interested in Eastern thought when he traveled to India and discovered Hindu teachings in 1965. Written as a recollected conversation, "Within You Without You" expresses the Western individualism belief that encourages separation and division: "With our love / We could save the world . . . / We're all one."[24]

U2's "One," written by Bono in the studio in fifteen minutes time, is an intense ballad about the pain of separation. The poetic message expressed in the song remains open to an assortment of interpretations. Some listeners may relate the number to relationships, while others interpret the lyrics to be about the band members themselves.

There are four songs on *Sgt. Pepper's* with salacious references to the time period's shifting youth culture and its illegal drug use. Martin claimed, "It was the beginning of the highly imaginative, some people might say, psychedelic way of writing."[25] The Beatles' producer was referring to "She's Leaving Home," "Within or Without You," the epic "A Day in the Life," and "Lucy in the Sky with Diamonds."

John had always insisted that "Lucy in the Sky with Diamonds" is a based on his four-year-old son's painting of a classmate, Lucy. He also claimed that the hallucinatory images in the song were inspired by the "Wool and Water" chapter in Lewis Carroll's *Through the Looking Glass*, and there is no connection to the song's initials, LSD, and the mind-altering drug. [26]

Sgt. Pepper's psychedelic numbers' connotations about love, mortality, and acid foreshadowed the "flower children" of the time. Certain singles' lyrics, such as references to having a smoke and "turn you on" in "A Day in the Life," got the single banned from many countries' radio stations. In 1968, Paul admitted that "A Day in the Life" was deliberately written to be provocative. "What we want to do is turn you on to the truth rather than on to pot," Martin later explained.[27]

According to John, the public will always consider *Sgt. Pepper's* to be the Beatles' acid album, but they had experienced LSD by the time *Revolver* was recorded in the summer of 1966. Martin explained the work environment that surrounded *Sgt. Pepper's*: "People often remember or talk about the drug taking during the sessions, but I never took drugs. It wasn't until much later that I found out that George used to put drugs in my coffee to keep me awake."[28]

Paul was well known for his connection to grass. In the 1970s, he was arrested several times for growing marijuana on his Scottish farm. The "cute Beatle" who sang *Sgt. Pepper's* "When I'm Sixty-Four" in 1967 turned sixty-four on June 18, 2006. "When I'm Sixty-Four" almost didn't wind up on *Sgt. Pepper's*. Originally, it was targeted as the flip side of "Strawberry Fields," but "Penny Lane" was chosen instead.

"Fixing a Hole" applies to all middle-class listeners, as the tune refers to simple home improvement. In 1967, Paul explained that the number has nothing to do with needles or heroin. Rather, "Fixing a Hole" is about adding color to a dry situation.[29]

Unlike *Sgt. Pepper's* material, U2 ceases to disguise any drug references in *Achtung Baby*'s lyrics. Rather, U2's singer mentions drugs as a metaphor for love gone sour. A woman is Bono's poison. In "So Cruel," he expresses, "Danger the drug that takes you higher." However, *Achtung Baby* is very straightforward with indications to illicit sex. In "Until the End of the World," a single about betrayal, Bono sings, "In my dream I was drowning my sorrows / But my sorrows, they learned to swim. / Surrounding me, / Going down on me / Spilling over the brim."

It has been forty years since its release, and *Sgt. Pepper's* is still considered by many the best album that the English-speaking world has ever seen. Yet the record's vivid imagery does not compare to U2's poetry. In "Tryin' to Throw Your Arms Around the World," Bono discusses a "Sunrise like a nosebleed," referring to the morning sky's color, as well as the stinging pain a man feels when waking up alone. Also, the song's simile, "And a woman needs a man / Like a fish needs a bicycle," sums up the entire album's creative and dark verses about love. *Achtung Baby* is not only U2's best LP, but it remains the best release of the past twenty years. Perhaps the essential U2 record would cease to exist if not for the creative and precarious expressions about love that stemmed from the Beatles' *Sgt. Pepper's Lonely Hearts Club Band.*

Records of a Generation: Twenty-first Century
The Beatles' *1* and U2's *The Best of 1980–1990*

In 2000, the staying power of the Beatles was proved yet again with the compilation of their greatest hits, properly titled *1*. During the time that the Beatles were recording for Parlaphone, Capitol, and Apple Records, they reached the top of both the American and British charts an overwhelming twenty-seven times. The album *1* brings the foursome's top-selling hits into digitally remastered collection. The album was pieced together in London's Abbey Road Studios, and includes liner notes by George Martin on the Beatles' remarkable evolution. There is even a thirty-page color insert that documents jacket artwork for each of the Beatles' most recognized singles. The eighty-minute compendium was a huge success throughout the commercial markets across the globe.

Just two years prior to The Beatles' *1* hitting stores, U2 released *The Best of 1980–1990*, with no regard to which numbers actually reached the top position on the sales charts. The band grew in stature with each new title on their eight albums. The sixty-minute package includes a limited-edition CD of B-sides of those early singles. The collection grossed $13.6 million worldwide.

Early teenybopper material introduces the Beatles' dominance of pop music in the 1960s. The enormously successful material on *1* includes "Love Me Do," which was recorded with session drummer Andy White. George Martin insisted that the Beatles needed a substitute on percussion in order to sound more professional, and "Love Me Do," an extraordinary synthesis of R&B, rock, and gospel, became the band's first hit in Britain for a week in 1962. Written by Paul and John, it was special because recording artists in the early 1960s rarely penned their own material. Interestingly, George had a black eye during the making of "Love Me Do" after ex-Beatles drummer Pete Best's fans attacked him in a bar.

Unlike *1*, *The Best of 1980–1990* does not place its tracks in chorological order. "Pride (In the Name of Love)," the song about Dr. Martin Luther King Jr., is off of 1984's *The Unforgettable Fire*. The song was actually released in advance of the poetic and emotional album, receiving noteworthy airplay on America's radio stations. "Pride (In the Name of Love)" cracked the UK Top 5 at number three and the US Top 40 at thirty-three.

"I Want to Hold Your Hand" stood at the States' top position for seven weeks in the spring of 1964, and stands as the gateway to the British Invasion. Rather than breaking into the US charts with teenybopper singles, U2's *War* record dealt with true-to-life political hardships and violent injustices, as is the case with "Sunday Bloody Sunday." The single, which reached number seven in the US charts, is a protest song against the armed forces in Northern Ireland who shot dead a dozen unarmed men and women at a football match. U2's lyrics are far more meaningful and complex than the early Beatles' hit.

U2's first recognition from the market came with the 1983 record *War*. Its initial single, "New Year's Day," is about the communist regime in Poland. The song made America's Top 100 chart at number fifty-three, as well as the UK's Top 10 for the first time.

The Beatles' "From Me to You" never entered the States' Top 40. However, it did reach number one on the British charts. Opposing the Beatles' joyous love, U2 recorded a ballad about a tangled web of complex anxieties. *The Joshua Tree*'s single from 1987, "With or Without You," expresses a man's doubt and guilt. Though it only made number four on the UK singles chart, "With or Without You" soared to the number one position in the States' *Billboard* listing.

On July 1, 1963, "She Loves You" was recorded in a single day. George's jazzy riffs and the opening chorus certainly show that the band was way ahead of its time. Similarly, the Irishmen's skills in elegant construction of songs came across in "I Still Haven't Found What I'm Looking For." The couplet from *The Joshua Tree* possesses obvious roots in gospel. Similar to "With or Without You," "I Still Haven't Found What I'm Looking For" went to number one in America but only number six in the United Kingdom. Sticking with the churchlike sound, "Angel of Harlem" was written on the road during the Joshua Tree Tour, and its Memphis horns shook the UK singles chart to number nine, and the US *Billboard* to number fourteen.

During one of the five weeks that "Can't Buy Me Love" claimed the *Billboard* winning slot in 1964, the Beatles held all five top spots on the US chart. The number two position was "Twist and Shout," followed by "She Loves You," "I Want to Hold Your Hand," and "Please Please Me." American inspirations, from Elvis Presley to Little Richard, can be heard throughout "Can't Buy Me Love." On the opposite end of the spectrum, U2 stuck to writing about human hardships. "Bad," off of 1984's *The Unforgettable Fire*, addresses heroin addiction. The drug problem was particularly prevalent in Dublin in the mid-1980s. During the Unforgettable Fire Tour, Bono would wrap a microphone cable around his arm in imitation of a junkie looking to shoot up.

Written in 1964 as the opening scene in the first Beatles film, *A Hard Day's Night*, the single of the same name reached number one in the States. Similarly, "Ticket to Ride" was a number one cut from the Beatles' second movie, *Help!* in the spring of 1965. The song is also the band's first on a recording to last over three minutes. John claimed it as "one of the earliest heavy-metal records."[30] Coincidently, "Ticket to Ride" was recorded on the same day that Lennon passed his British driver's exam. The first release from U2's 1988 major motion picture, *Rattle and Hum* was "Desire." The band's American rhythm and blues influence is evident and it reached number three on the American *Billboard* chart and number one in the United Kingdom.

Before Hendrix turned metallic noise into art, Lennon accidentally created guitar feedback through his amplifier in October of 1964. The mistake was used as the introduction to "I Feel Fine," becoming a pinnacle point in the evolution of rock and roll. The single was released that winter and sat at number one for three weeks in the United States, five in the United Kingdom. Similarly, the Beatles' experimental sounds in the opening of "Eight Days a Week," and their double-tracked vocals, can be directly compared with U2's "Where the Streets Have No Name." The variation of the introductory chords took weeks of frustrating work in U2's studio. The song contains a message of breaking away to anonymity but never states the location that the lyrics are describing. "Where the Streets Have No Name" didn't trek higher than number thirteen in America but rode to number four on the other side of the Atlantic.

All of the *Rattle and Hum* tracks are bunched together at the end of U2's first greatest hits disc. "When Love Comes to Town" is the band's collaboration with American blues legend B. B. King, who opened for the Irish band on the Joshua Tree Tour. "When Love Comes to Town" fuses gospel with the blues' intense lyrics penned by Bono. Reaching number six in the United Kingdom, the ditty only hit number sixty-eight in the States. B. B. King was still performing the single regularly on his 2006 tour, even if U2 has denied their concertgoers the song in the new millennium.

As B. B. King points out in the film, Bono writes extremely "heavy" lyrics. For example, "The Unforgettable Fire," from the 1984 record of the same name, was written about the atomic bombs dropped on Hiroshima and Nagasaki during World War II and the immediate death toll. The single didn't gain much respect in the US market, but it climbed to number six on the UK singles chart. Also, "I Will Follow," the only single from 1980's *Boy* to be included on *The Best of 1980–1990*, is about a child's yearning after experiencing separation anxiety from his mother. True, it took a few years on the market, but "I Will Follow" peaked at number eighty-one on the US *Billboard* listing in 1984. Written for his wife, Ali, "The Sweetest Thing" is Bono's sweet expression of desperation for his mate. The song was omitted from *The Joshua Tree* but reappeared on *The Best of 1980–1990*. The pop-like, upbeat original version of "The Sweetest Thing" first appeared in 1987 as the B-side of the "Where the Streets Have No Name" single.

Sincerity is evident on *1* as well. A chart-topper in 1965, "Help!" amounts to Lennon's personal cry about the overwhelming success of his career. "I could talk to you about 'Help!,' because we did a version of it," explained Bono in 2001. "It's obvious what it's all about, and when I sang it, I needed to. 'Help!' just became a real prayer."[31] "Day Tripper," the complex arrangement about the habitual use of hallucinogenics, was recreated onstage every night of the Beatles' final concert trek in 1966. Although "Day Tripper" topped the charts for five weeks in the United Kingdom during the winter of 1965, it never climbed higher than number five in the States. A few weeks earlier "Yesterday" stood at number one in the states. The mature ballad conceived entirely by Paul has grown into one of the most covered songs in rock history.

Written on the road during the Joshua Tree Tour, "Angel of Harlem" shook the UK singles chart to number nine, and the US *Billboard* to number fourteen. The harmonies of the Beatles' love song "We Can Work It Out" made number one in America for three weeks in January of 1966. Meanwhile, *Rattle and Hum*'s "All I Want Is You" is a ballad about commitment. The lyrics express the generosity of spirit that Bono's wife possesses for him. "All I Want Is You" became the fourth-best-selling single in the United Kingdom for a week in 1989, and reached number eighty-three in America.

In 2002, U2 gave listeners *The Best of 1990–2000*. The superstars responded to their second decade with creativity. True, half the number of the 1980s songs were cut, but as the U2 anthology chronicles, they managed to produce a memorable, lasting body of work in a time when grunge ruled the airwaves and cable television stations. *Achtung Baby*, *Zooropa*, and *Pop* yielded timeless material, as well as singles from seductive soundtracks.

The summer of 1966 had "Paperback Writer" at the top of the charts for a couple of weeks. The vigorous thumping of Ringo's bass drum introduces the Beatles' psychedelic stage, while the single is the band's first number one that is not a love song. Similarly, twenty-five years later, *Achtung Baby* brought about U2's experimental electronica for the new age's rave scene. The first cut on U2's *The Best of 1990–2000* is the dance floor–friendly "Even

Better than the Real Thing," which only climbed to number thirty-two in America, but reached number eight in the United Kingdom. Coca-Cola had been using "The Real Thing" as an advertising slogan, and U2 turned down a high-paying offer to use the single in Virgin Cola commercials.

Less than two months after "Paperback Writer" dropped from the number one position in the United Kingdom, "Yellow Submarine" emerged at the top. Ringo's monotone provided the simple narrative of an amusing children's number about a sailor beneath the waves. The single sparked an animated film and loads of psychedelic art, despite the song's lack of drug references. Similarly, the Edge and his lifeless vocals are featured on *Zooropa's* "Numb." Written entirely and sung by the guitarist, Bono sings only the high-pitched chorus of the poetic messages set to arcade music. The playful animation of "Yellow Submarine" can also be directly compared with U2's lighthearted cartoon video utilizing humor for "Hold Me, Thrill Me, Kiss Me, Kill Me." The single was originally intended for *Zooropa* but didn't appear on the market until the *Batman Forever* soundtrack in 1995. Peaking at number sixteen in the United States, "Hold Me, Thrill Me, Kiss Me, Kill Me" got to number two on the UK singles chart.

Zooropa's "The First Time," a song about losing all faith, was featured on the soundtrack to the 2000 movie *The Million Dollar Hotel*. It was influenced directly by soul singer Al Green. During the third verse, it ditches its symmetry and ads a fresh twist to it. U2 never played "The First Time" live until 2005's Vertigo tour. It stands as the first time a number was performed after it did not appear on the tour to support an album, the Zooropa leg of the Zoo TV Tour.

"Mysterious Ways" is an upbeat, optimistic single about all women in general being superior to men. The track features a funky dance framework. It was a massive success, reaching number nine in the States and thirteen across the pond. The belly dancer, who was featured in a video filmed in Morocco, also performed live onstage during *Achtung Baby's* Zoo TV tour. The illustrious dancer, Morleigh Steinberg, later married the Edge.

Zooropa tour, *photo by Sean McClotsky*

"Eleanor Rigby" never made it to number one in the States but did reign in the United Kingdom for four weeks. Though three of the Beatles sing on the record, none of the band's instrumentation can be heard in this character-driven story. The striking lyrics, about the loneliness of old age, display the transformation from a pop-oriented act to a more serious and experimental studio band.

Paul recollected memories of his childhood in Liverpool and wrote about a traffic circle known as "Penny Lane." Paul and John grew up in the area, and they spent a lot of time playing on Penny Lane as kids. The barber shop mentioned is owned by a Mr. Bioletti, who has claimed to have cut hair for Paul, John, and George when they were children. The autobiographical single reached number one in the United Kingdom for one week in 1967.

U2 dipped into *Zooropa* and *Pop* for their strongest material and remixed some older songs into a fresh dance mix known as "Electrical Storm." Recorded for the second greatest hits album, it tells the tale of quarrelling lovers, relating the high tension between them to a looming cyclone. U2 has never performed

"Electrical Storm" live. "The Hands that Built America" is the last single recorded for *The Best of 1990–2000*. Two years later, it was used in Martin Scorsese's *Gangs of New York* soundtrack. The contribution was nominated for Best Original Song Written for a Motion Picture, but U2 lost to Eminem's "Lose Yourself." Despite the film's setting in the mid-1800s, the lyrics to "The Hands that Built America" reference the September 11, 2001, World Trade Center attacks: "It's early fall, there's a cloud on the New York skyline."

Written for the *Our World* television special in the summer of 1967, the Beatles orchestrated "All You Need Is Love." The simple chorus about flower power earned a number one position in the States for a week in August. "I don't think all that kind of flowers-in-the-hair stuff ever sat well with the Beatles," explained Bono in 2001. "They were four hard men from Liverpool so when they start thinking about love, it's a harder love. It's about the imagination, that you have to *imagine* something before you can make it so."[32]

Giving proceeds to the War Child charity to help harassed Bosnians survive against the advancing Serbs, U2 released "Miss Sarajevo" in 1995. Joined by guest vocalist Luciano Pavarotti, it contains Italian lyrics. On the same note, the Fab Four sing "Geh Raus," or "Get Back" in Italian, on one of their *Rarities* collections. The song from 1969 symbolizes the Beatles returning to their original rock sound. In the States, the song reigned the charts for five weeks. "Get Back" is the only Beatles single to enter the UK listing at number one, a position held for six weeks. It is also the Beatles' first single to be released in true stereo instead of mono, and was the last number the four performed together in public at the unannounced rooftop gig on January 30, 1969.

Not unlike "Geh Raus," U2 left behind their hip-hop dance gurus and returned to their basics with 2000's *All That You Can't Leave Behind*. The album's first single, "Beautiful Day," achieved number one in Norway, Canada, and the United Kingdom, despite peaking at twenty-one in the States. Combining 1950s' doo-wop with spiritual electronics, the beautiful song turned into a momentous U2 anthem and picked up a Grammy Award.

In the winter of 1968, the Beatles recorded "Lady Madonna" as an ode to womanhood. The piano and saxophone segments were intended as a tribute to Fats Domino, who achieved his last Top 40 hit when he covered it later that year. "Lady Madonna" stands as the last Beatles record to be released on the Parlophone label in the United Kingdom and the Capitol label in the United States before the formation of the Beatles' famous Apple Records. The business umbrella for the boys' merchandise also signed James Taylor and Billy Preston to its label.

Ringing in the New Year, 1967, "Hello, Goodbye" possessed the US number one position for three weeks. According to George Martin, the chanting in the song's conclusion led to the melody heard later in "Hey Jude."[33] The king of Beatles singles in America remains "Hey Jude," as it sat at number one for nine weeks in the winter of 1968. Originally titled "Hey Julian," it's Paul's offering of comfort to John's son during John's divorce from Cynthia Lennon. Of course, the name was changed to make it more sonically pleasing.

Lennon turned his autobiography into a high-spirited comedy for listeners to soak up. "The Ballad of John and Yoko" reached number one in the United Kingdom but didn't climb higher than number eight in America during the summer of '69. On a more serious level, George penned the serene love song "Something" for his wife Patti, and that hit the UK's number one for a week in October of 1969. "When I wrote it, in my mind I heard Ray Charles singing it," Harrison expressed. "And he did do it some years later." George didn't care for Frank Sinatra's cover version, especially when the Chairman of the Board referred to it as his favorite Lennon/McCartney song.[34]

"One" is Bono's ballad about a guilty party in a recently squashed relationship. Whether it is romantic liaisons or the kinships between band members, the lyrics allow a wealth of possible meanings. The ambiguity has popularized the song, allowing for many different interpretations. Galgalatz, an Israeli radio station, ranked "One" as the best song of the twentieth century. It has been covered by legendary artists Johnny Cash and Joe Cocker. "One" made number seven in the United Kingdom and number ten on the United States *Billboard* listing.

Modeled after Chuck Berry's "You Can't Catch Me," "Come Together" hit number one in the United States for a week in November of 1969. Lennon created the lyrics to the funky blues track in the recording studio that summer. The song has since become a heavily covered tune, as Aerosmith, Michael Jackson, Soundgarden, Axl Rose, and Bruce Springsteen have all recreated their own versions.

"Stay (Faraway, So Close!)," off of 1993's *Zooropa*, allows plenty of space for poetic interpretations. For example, it is up to the listener to figure out if the woman who appears "out of a hole in the ground" is a stranger, a friend, or a lover. Grasping number four on the UK singles chart, "Stay (Faraway, So Close!)" was left at number sixty-one on the US *Billboard*.

Bono wrote "Stuck in a Moment You Can't Get Out Of" in response to his Australian friend, Michael Hutchence of INXS, being found dead. Bono believed the cause of death was suicide, rather than asphyxiation during a risqué autoerotic experience. The song is putting Hutchence in his place for not possessing the backbone to deal with life's challenges. "Stuck in a Moment You Can't Get out Of" hit number two in the United Kingdom but never passed number fifty-two in the States. Similarly, "Gone," a punk rocker's dance single off of 1997's *Pop* release, was often dedicated to the late Hutchence on the PopMart tour.

On *Achtung Baby*'s dark "Until the End of the World" Bono discusses his own life from a pessimist's perspective: sex, love, spirituality with Jesus, and mistrust of man. The song is also used in the soundtrack to the *Until the End of the World* movie. Set in the futurist society of 1999, the 1991 film entails a fugitive couple on the from the CIA; they span the globe, eventually ending up in Australia with a device that records one's dreams.

"Discotheque" was the first single released off of *Pop*. The fast-paced dance track can be understood as a message about drugs, as well the physical pleasures of sex. As usual, "Discotheque" sold extremely better in the United Kingdom, reaching number one, but never passed number ten on US *Billboard* listing. *Pop*'s next single, "Staring at the Sun," was influenced by the British Invasion's Kinks. Bono's personal poetry entails self-mockery while being lazy on a Sunday afternoon. "Staring at the Sun" reached number twenty-six in the United States and three on the UK singles chart.

The Beatles' "Let It Be" was number one for a couple of weeks in April 1970 in the United States. The track was recorded during high tensions. Although some listeners believe it is a hymn to the Virgin Mary, "Let It Be"was written as Paul's tribute to his mother, Mary, who died when he was fourteen.

"The Long and Winding Road" is the Beatles' chart-topping swan song, sitting as a US number one for two weeks in the summer of 1970. After the recording sessions, producer Phil Spector remixed the melancholy song using eighteen violins, four violas, four cellos, three trumpets, three trombones, two guitars, and a choir of fourteen women. Paul heard the new version and was outraged. Nine days later, McCartney announced to the world that he was leaving the Beatles.

Unbelievably, "The Fly" is not on *The Best of 1990–2000*. Even though the single did not pass number sixty-one on the US charts, fans cannot fathom why *Achtung Baby*'s first release, introducing the new industrial sounds of U2 in the early '90s, was passed over. On the Zoo TV Tour, Bono dressed as the Fly persona, a leather-clad rock star wearing huge sunglasses and making phone calls to President George H. W. Bush. Perhaps the band's marketing team had their reasons.

For the most part, each of the singles contained on the Beatles' *1* and U2's *The Best of* albums sold better in the United Kingdom than the United States. The Beatles' *1* moved 3.6 million copies in its first week and more than 12 million in three weeks worldwide, becoming the fastest-selling album of all time. The Beatles collection also hit diamond certification, as it sold ten million copies in the States. It is the sixth Beatles album to reach such a plateau, breaking their tie with Led Zeppelin in that department. The songs making up the Beatles' *1* and U2's *The Best of* spark memories of screaming teens for both baby boomers and their children.

6

Concerts of a Generation

WHILE *SGT. PEPPER'S* was created with the intention of never being performed, the Beatles took American culture by storm with their first tour of the States in the summer and fall of 1964. Virtually every one of these shows, including gigs throughout Europe, America, Hong Kong, Japan, Australia, and New Zealand, sold out in no time. The Beatles' road trip established the concept of rock concerts in a stadium, playing to tens of thousands of delirious fans. Of course, each venue was considerably smaller than U2's present-day affairs. The biggest bands of the following two decades, including the Rolling Stones, the Who, Pink Floyd, and the mighty Led Zeppelin, followed the Beatles' example and began to continually conquer massive outdoor arenas on global tours.

Since 1991's Zoo TV, U2 has presented rock and roll as a spectacle in the cultures' enormous venues around the globe, utilizing "a mass of technical, aesthetic and theatrical devices."[1] The goal of the festive shows was to add to the concert experience, as well as the meaning of the music. In March 2001, a new U2 tour kicked off in South Florida. *All that You Can't Leave Behind*'s Elevation tour in 2001, sponsored by MTV and VH1, consisted of multiple dates in thirty-three North American cities. This was the band's first tour in ten years in which all the venues were indoors. The intimate show was also the first in U2's rich history to be physically smaller than its predecessor, earning the band a load of publicity. In the March 2001 edition of *Rolling Stone*, U2's guitarist claimed that "music is going to be the [Elevation Tour's] centerpiece. As a band, we're always looking for a magic that occurs when we play with our audience present. That's why people come back to U2 shows time and again."[2]

For the Elevation Tour, Ticketmaster and U2 left open the option of adding more dates for American venues that quickly sold out, as was the case in sixteen cities, including Miami/Ft. Lauderdale, Los Angeles, and Atlanta. U2 was still at the peak of their game in Europe as well. Three different concerts in Germany sold out in under an hour, and fifty thousand seats for a Holland gig were grabbed in thirty minutes. Eventually, there were zero unsold seats for every stop on the continent. Eight shows in London sold out as well. U2's success with the Elevation tour was partially due to four different MTV videos and one rooftop concert, in the spirit of the Beatles' last performance together on top of a London building.

According to journalist Larry Kane, the Beatles concerts in 1964 were "plain and simple."[3] The band was electric, performing with true excitement, harmony, and grace. Similarly, *RAG Magazine* reported on U2's simple approach of going "back to the basics."[4] U2 had a more stripped down stage when they kicked off the Elevation tour on March 24, 2001, in South Florida's National Car Rental Center, later known as the American Airlines Arena. U2 had ditched the electronic rhythms of their 1997 tour and moved back to the guitar-driven sound of its youth, not unlike the Beatles' *Let It Be* three years after the stimulating *Sgt. Pepper's*.

On September 2, 1964, the Beatles performed in front of a mostly white audience of thirteen thousand in Philadelphia's Convention Hall, as the city had undergone race riots earlier in the

Bono, Miami, 2001, *photo by Sean McCloskey*

week. The sight disgusted the four musicians. As a result, the Beatles made a stink during a press conference in Toronto five days later. The four threatened to walk off the stage in a protest in Jacksonville, Florida's Gator Bowl the following week if the concert wouldn't be open to all colors.

"We never play to segregated audiences and we're not going to start now," John explained to the American press. "I'd rather lose our appearance money. We understand that in Florida they only allow for Negroes to sit in the balconies at performances, but we will not appear unless Negroes are allowed to sit anywhere they like."[5] The protest against a segregated venue worked, but few black fans were interested in seeing the Beatles perform.

Expressing the theme of equality to the global culture's youth, U2 wrote a number about civil rights. "MLK" appeared in the film *Rattle and Hum* in 1988. "And when Martin Luther King talked about the dream, he was not just talking about the American dream, he was talking about something much bigger," Bono declared when accepting an International Freedom Award in October 2004. "He was talking about equality in the rest of the world."[6]

Most of the Beatles' shows were utter bedlam, as hundreds of exhausted kids ended up sprawled out on the ground due to the hysteria. In Seattle, sailors assisted police in fending off kids who broke through police lines. At many venues, nurses carried out dozens of girls who had fainted in order to administer oxygen to them. Of course, the fact that a great many unruly fans threw jelly beans inside Carnegie Hall, and other halls where the band appeared, did not help. The police interrupted many of the shows, hoping to get the message across that the jelly beans were dangerous.

According to Larry Kane, George was the culprit after telling a New York newspaper that his bandmates were stealing his "jelly babies," a much softer version of jelly beans sold in England.[7] In Keith Badman's book, *The Beatles Off the Record*, John was blamed after the Big Apple's press reported his quote, "George had eaten all my jelly babies."[8]

"That night, we were absolutely pelted by the fuckin' things," George later explained about the hectic Beatles show. "To make matters worse, we were on a circular stage, so they hit us from all sides. *Imagine* waves of rock-hard little bullets raining down on you from the sky. It's a bit dangerous, you know, 'cos if a jelly bean, traveling about fifty miles an hour through the air, hits you in the eye, you're finished."[9]

On the other hand, many of Elevation's write-ups are quite similar. In April of 2001, *RAG* discussed the Edge's live performance. "The guitarist touched us with the settling back in his control of the 'cha cha.' The Edge was the driving force reaching us with melodic rhythmic patterns."[10] A couple of months later, *Spin* magazine's Nick Marino reported on the Edge's "melody-oriented playing [that] continues to chime like church bells."[11]

Dennis Sheridan was fourteen years old when he took a bus and a train to see the Beatles at Shea Stadium. The crowd was mostly children and few drove to the ballpark. The tickets at Shea were $5.75 apiece. It was not like seeing a Mets game or a concert these days in Queens, as there was no partying or tailgating outside the venue, nor were there T-shirt vendors. Sheridan contests that both boys and girls were screaming so loud that he couldn't hear the

Bono and the Edge, *photo by Sean McCloskey*

Beatles whatsoever, but simply attending the historical event was momentous enough.

It's a fact that U2's crowd in 2001 was a little older and more respectful than 1964's candy-pelting spectators. The Beatles' concertgoers were generally thousands of crazed teenagers, mainly screaming girls, on the band's first American road trip in 1964. But their August 23 gig in the Hollywood Bowl consisted of more reserved adults among the seventeen thousand caucasians. On the reverse side, all colors and ages ranging from fifteen to fifty dressed up for each presentation of U2's Elevation.

The 1964 concerts featured the Bill Black Combo, Jackie De Shannon, and the Righteous Brothers as the opening acts. Meanwhile Elevation's opener in North America was not the originally billed PJ Harvey. Rather, the Corrs, who left their homeland of Ireland breathless after selling over sixteen million records, opened for U2.

Before the main attraction, U2 fans waved their Irish flags throughout Elevation's arenas. Each concert consisted of a simple heart walkway wrapping around the stage. Standing admissions surrounded both sides of the heart, making the stage itself the key to the entire concert. This clever device projected intimacy, while allowing Bono and the band to delve deep into the arena and truly face each section of the stadium. The stage was nothing like 1991's extravagant Zoo TV, or the surreal PopMart extravaganza. In the book *U2 Live*, Pimm Jal De La Parra cleverly wrote, "It's like chopping down *The Joshua Tree* all over again, there's not a lemon in sight."[12]

Almost four decades earlier, the Beatles were forced to reposition their own equipment three separate times to allow each fan a decent view. Unlike the Beatles' setup in New York's Shea Stadium, U2 had giant projectors displaying the band for those elevated in the stands. Perhaps the greatest of the amenities in almost every venue was that they sold Guinness Stout—Ireland's second great contribution to American culture.[13]

The Dublin band kicked off the Elevation journey with all of the lights on at five minutes after nine p.m. Forty-year-old Bono led the timeless band onto the stage. The lead singer slowly strutted in his trademark outfit of black leather and sunglasses, and the Edge flaunted a classic old-school Miami Dolphins T-shirt with his black skullcap, unlike the Beatles' matching suits and mop-top hairdos in 1964. In Shea

Elevation ticket stub

Stadium, a helicopter landed on the field at eight thirty and the crowd went nuts as John led the Fab Four to the stage. The Beatles dove straight into "Twist and Shout."

U2's audience erupted every night as Bono announced "Alright" into the mic and U2 shot into "Elevation." The Grammy-winning "Beautiful Day" was played second, building on the heartbeat thump of the number's verse. The swarming general-admission crowd waved their arms to Bono as he strutted to the back of the arena on his heart-shaped runway; a singing bird on a concrete stage.

Larry, who had not changed his hairstyle in over twenty years, very un-Fab, set the pace with his steady foot on the bass drum. A yellow searchlight followed Bono as he danced around the heart-shaped walkway. The giant black-and-white screen over the stage displayed Larry banging away on his drums. The prop was no different from the Beatles' gig in Shea Stadium, where a video camera captured Ringo and caused "an explosion of squealing."[14]

During "Until the End of the World," Bono circled the heart, touching fans, before he collapsed onto his back. Always desperate to communicate and connect with his audience, Bono dislocated his shoulder after falling off a scaffold in 1987. His manager has since forbidden the stuntman to climb onstage. The Beatles did not usually jump around, as their movements onstage were quite minimal. John, an incredible showman, was the most enthusiastic, nodding, winking, and smiling to the audience during "I Want to Hold Your Hand."

While a blue light shined over the Edge's keyboard solo in "New Year's Day," Bono walked to the back of the stage to wave to the fans with an obstructed view. He also sang the decent melody "Stuck in a Moment." It was not the most enthralling song of the evening, as many concertgoers took the time for a bathroom break. Such a maneuver was not even thinkable during any of the Beatles' short shows.

U2 stripped to the bare essentials on Elevation, very Beatles-like, when they performed three songs from *Pop*. Each number was given a fresher appeal by trimming the fat and cutting all of the scenic bullshit from PopMart, the least aesthetically successful U2 tour in years. During South Florida's two shows, Bono talked about the making of the *Pop* album on Miami's distinguished South Beach before executing "Discotheque." Only a select few of Elevation's stops heard the crashing bash of Zeppelin's epic "Whole Lotta Love" mixed into the number. "Staring at the Sun" and "New York" reached the thousands of screaming Irish, Italian, Jewish, Hispanic, and black fans in the arena. Such a multicultural collection did not really exist on the Beatles' 1964 and 1965 American tours.

Fifteen minutes into every Beatles concert in 1964 and '65, the crowd's misconduct got more attention than the Beatles themselves. As Larry Kane experienced, men and women of all shapes and ages were pressed together on their chairs, "screaming, moaning, groaning, ripping at their hair, pushing, shoving, falling on the floor and crying, real tears streaming down hundreds of faces, smearing their mascara and lipstick."[15]

The self-proclaimed "last of the rock stars" stood stationary in front of the microphone, but this time with a guitar strapped on. U2 played a short, but passionate, three-minute version of their old-school ditty "I Will Follow" before the grandiose number "Sunday Bloody Sunday." Bono once claimed that it's "the first song that ever got me into trouble." During the straightforward number with no special effects, every fan was on his or her feet clapping and singing the familiar chorus, "How long? How long must we sing this song. . . ." In several North American venues, Bono meshed in twenty seconds of Bob Marley's "Get Up, Stand Up" into the non-rebel song. U2 has always respected the greats, covering songs by Elvis, Hendrix, B. B. King, and of course, the Beatles.

Night after night, the restless audience waited for U2 to pull selections from *Achtung Baby*. Bono always appeased. He sometimes began singing "Mysterious Ways" while lying on his back. The dancing silhouette of a belly dancer on the stage's screen reminded thousands of the illustrious video. According to Chris Cimaglia, an audio-recording technician, U2's altered pace in "The Fly," mixed with the weak acoustics of any indoor show, made the song seem confused and unrehearsed. "Not all of the instruments were in synch." The singer would often plummet into the stands and swim to the back of the floor's general admission area. It's no secret that Bono loves his job. Whereas Zoo TV is the equivalent of *Sgt. Pepper's* performed live in the world's most colossal outdoor stadiums, the more mature Elevation tour 2001 could have supported the legendary band's *Let It Be*.[16]

Although the Beatles' sets were far too brief to consider such an act, U2 always took a break. During most gigs, the four reemerged with "Bullet the Blue Sky." Bono held a bright light behind the

Edge as he paced around the giant heart. The created silhouette brought fans back to the cover of *Rattle and Hum*. Next, Bono turned the light to the stands, illuminating all the colors of a royal flush. The beam gave the sensation of a helicopter search party. Those old enough would have been reminded of the Beatles' entrance into Shea Stadium.

With "bodies lunging randomly," the Beatles' shows were always sure to wind down with policemen fighting fans in every part of the venue.[17] Thirty to forty minutes later, "All My Loving," "Long Tall Sally," and "Please Please Me" were all performed as the final numbers on the Beatles' first historic tour throughout the States. Always the showman, John once ignored a policeman's command to exit the stage. Larry Kane watched the Beatles perform a "little dance to sidestep the officer's hands while making faces at him."[18] The Fab Four always showed fan appreciation with bows. Next, the four musical messiahs would have to dash to safety. The authorities estimated that there were at least twenty thousand exuberant kids waiting to get a peek at any of their idols. On top of the lethal jelly beans, the Beatles sometimes had to dodge tin cans tossed from the stands.

U2 has never been a show-off band. Besides the iconic singer, no individual stood out in any of the Elevation Tour's numbers, as they are all equally fantastic. The Edge didn't need to play any hair-raising, finger-tapping solos. The guitarist's beauty lies in his melodic and rhythmic delay. Neither Adam nor Larry stood out by doing anything special with their instruments, probably because the two low-key musicians have never been the front men onstage. And no, Bono never flaunted his infamous devil's horns from Pop-Mart. He kept his humanitarian lectures down to a minimum as well. More reserved in 2001, the U2 concert was no longer an electric smorgasbord like a car crash. The Elevation tour was utterly amazing throughout North America.

The Beatles' massive outdoor concert at Shea Stadium was engineered by Clair Brothers Audio,[19] the first to make Elvis heard in arenas. The hysteria bred by fifty-five thousand screeching Beatles fans plagued the sound of the amplifiers and the minute house system.

The Beatles' 1964 experience in New York was a turning point that encouraged the development of bigger and stronger PA systems.

Any closed arena is sonically degrading to a live performance. On today's touring circuit, a great band, such as U2, makes a concertgoer forget about the acoustical problems associated with such venues. John Lennon once described the sound in "San Francisco's Carnegie Hall" as horrible. "The acoustics were terrible and. . . . It wasn't a rock show; it was just a sort of circus where we were in cages. . . . We were just like animals."[20]

The way the Beatles fans across the country defied authority is quite memorable. Crowds of middle-class kids forging ahead and piercing police lines had been rare in the '50s. The almost sexual openness of the crowd was also startling. Suddenly, normal, polite teenagers were showing their passion and pleasure in a very public way. This was shocking to an older generation, but sensuality was replacing sensibility, and the road was opening to an expanded liberation. The impact of the Beatles' style on their fans, too, was enormous. The haircut that many adopted to copy the band was especially notable. The fashion looked primitive by today's standards, but it was a precursor of the long-haired look that would soon accompany the antiwar protests.

For Elevation tour's swan song, U2 executed *All That You Can't Leave Behind*'s "Walk On." The media giants each waived and gave a bow with practically zero disrespect from the stands. U2's finale, a hundred and twenty minutes since their initial appearance each night, always consisted of people honoring the band members with claps, cheers, and whistles. Though perhaps not to the extent of Shea Stadium's life-changing audio technology or memoirs of the Beatles, it was nonetheless thrilling to see 2001's biggest band in the world perform in indoor arenas. From "Beautiful Day" to "Mysterious Ways" and "One," the Elevation Tour reconfirmed U2's status, once again, as cultural icons.

What ought to be realized is that when U2 went back to their roots recording *All That You Can't Leave Behind*, they went too far. Besides one beautiful song, the album is boring, and the musicians' sound unchallenged. But the 2001 trek was quite the

Bono and Adam, *photo by Sean McCloskey*

opposite. The simple approach to writing on the new album came across as refreshing in a live arena. The band and the thousands of fans were captivated each night of U2's Elevation tour. That was the big idea.

The Beatles' first US tours in 1964 and 1965 changed American society, as the youth were led in a new direction in music, clothing, hairstyles, and vocabulary. Those performances represented more than a pop show. The events were all-encompassing, once-in-a-lifetime experiences that few fans are fortunate to share. The Beatles undoubtedly led a revolution, upping society's expectations of live performances, even if it was that *rock-and-roll music.*

2005 Concerts of a Generation

All over the world baby boomers and their children gathered by the thousands to experience Paul McCartney's 2005 global jaunt. The icon headed through North America to promote his critically acclaimed *Chaos and Creation in the Backyard,* Paul's twentieth

Sean's Sir Paul, *photo by Sean McCloskey*

release, which hit stores in September 2005. His band, Wings, broke records for ticket sales on their 1976 world trek, and Paul's previous venture was the top profiting tour of 2002. The rock star earned $103.3 million in 2005, with ticket prices soaring into the hundreds. Yet, McCartney's 2005 journey was not the biggest money-making tour of the year, as its span was minuscule compared to the Rolling Stones, the Eagles, and U2.

On the road at the same time as Sir Paul, U2's Vertigo tour made its way across the globe in support of *How to Dismantle an Atomic Bomb*. Before 2005 was up, U2 sold out more than a hundred indoor-arena and stadium shows around the world and performed for 3.2 million screaming fans. The Stones came in first at the box office, earning $162 million. Meanwhile,

Sir Paul ticket stub

Sir Paul took home a humble $56 million. The artists can also earn as much as $150,000 a night from merely the merchandise sold.

Led by Zeppelin's tour manager, Dennis Sheehan, U2 sold out every one of their twenty-four arena shows. The lack of tickets available was no surprise, as U2 has moved over 8.5 million copies worldwide of their 2004 release, *How to Dismantle an Atomic Bomb*. Entertaining more than 420,000 spectators

U2 Denver ticket stub

with twenty-five years' worth of material, U2 earned over $40 million in ticket sales in 2005 alone. Though prices remained high, the average U2 ticket, at $120, did not compare to what Sir Paul was getting.

Rather than sharing a bill, Paul ran a ten-minute video documentary on his career at each of the sold-out arenas of almost twenty thousand Beatles and McCartney fans. "McCartney doesn't really do opening acts," Paul's lead guitarist, Rusty Anderson, explained at the Miami engagement. "He's had pre-show conceptual things, but never really rock bands playing." Meanwhile, the Kings of Leon opened for the U2 in 2005.

U2's audience was almost always a respectful crowd, anywhere between the ages of fifteen and fifty, who dressed like Gap kids for the social event. As expected, there was an enormous line for each performance's general-admission seating, which took up the entire floor of each arena. Meanwhile, seat holders walked on through the door. Like U2's 2001 show, a giant walkway circled the amphitheater, allowing the band to venture into the heart of the crowd, which was general admission. Underneath florescent chandeliers hung a galaxy of strobe lights, along with four video monitors, each with split screens devoted to each member of the band. Again, the madness of the 1990s' Zoo TV and PopMart multimedia extravaganzas was dropped and the concert revolved simply around the music, not unlike Paul's 2005 gig.

Utilizing forty years' worth of timeless material from the Quarrymen, the Beatles, Wings, and his solo career, Paul opened each concert with the Wings single "Jet." Throughout the 1970s, he did not appease his audiences with Beatles songs when he toured with his late wife, Linda. In 1985, Michael Jackson outbid Paul on the ownership rights to the heavenly Beatles catalog, and there was nothing he could say, say, say about it. But following the success of the anthologies in the mid-'90s, the classic material rocketed him to the position of the richest cat in England. That was until his young wife took him for a ride in 2006 after getting hitched without a prenuptial agreement. Beatles fans universally agree that Paul has to move forward as well as go back. Jackson has also agreed to sell his 50 percent holdings in Sony/ATV, as the man has massive legal fees of his own. The publishing company possesses the rights to more than 250 classics that are now worth over $1 billion.

Paul, the best-looking and greatest-sounding sixty-three-year-old that most concertgoers had ever seen, would dive straight into "Magical Mystery Tour." Psychedelic light arrangements and one enormous TV monitor added color to the simple set design. Paul and his guitar stood center stage every night, while four other musicians surrounded the artist. He wore black slacks and a blazer over a skintight turquoise shirt. Onstage, the "cute one" stood behind the mic, bobbing his head when he sang, recreating the matching-suit Beatles.

Similar to McCartney, the four members of U2 would kick things off nonchalantly, with no small talk, performing "City of Blinding Lights." The 2004 ballad was written about the Big Apple. The forty-five-year-old singer wore five inches of hair falling to his shoulder blades, black leather, and denim outfits, along with his Fly sunglasses. The Edge, draped in his trademark black skullcap, black T-shirt, and leather slacks, leaned on one knee, swinging to the rhythmic patterns of the music.

The first part of U2's concert was extremely fast-paced and contained recent material, as Bono announced, "Uno, Dos, Tres, Catorce," introducing *How to Dismantle*'s first single, "Vertigo."

With the exception of one guitar overdub in the conclusion, the track's bass, guitar, and drums were recorded in one take. Tens of thousands of fans sang the familiar chorus as the Irish boys played rock and rock.

On the opposite end of the spectrum, Paul began his shows with a few of the pre-Beatles cabaret-type pieces from the Quarrymen. Every night, the Englishman explained to his crowd that "Till There Was You" would get the band local gigs in Liverpool and was recorded in the small town of Kensington in 1958. As learned from following his 2002 Driving USA tour, Paul tells the same stories and one-liner jokes every night of the tour to his diehard fans, while refusing to change up his set-list.

The crowd hopped up and down in unison, throwing their arms toward Bono on his walkway during "Elevation." Upon finishing the number, Adam Clayton's bass kicked off a slower version of "Mysterious Ways." Facing the back of the stage, Bono's torso danced in slow motion during an extended exit, repeating, "She moves me, She moves me." During *The Joshua Tree* classic "I Still Haven't Found What I'm Looking For," Bono always let the thousands of fans sing the second verse before he finished the popular chorus.

During the Vertigo tour's highlight, "Beautiful Day," Bono sat on one knee as all the colors came out in the arena's light fixtures, alternating between red, blue, and yellow. He

Bono, Vertigo Tour, *photo by Sean McCloskey*

Bono, Vertigo Tour, *photo by Sean McCloskey*

waved slowly, concluding the number with the repetitive phrase "It's alright, it's alright" fading away into silence.

Meanwhile, *Abbey Road*'s "She Came in through the Bathroom Window" was a highlight for Paul's crowds, as well as Wings' multidimensional "Band on the Run." The complex arrangement, as opposed to the band's silly love songs, brought listeners back to the *Sgt. Pepper's Lonely Hearts Club Band* record; convenient, considering that Paul always followed the number with "Sgt. Pepper's."

The greatest addition to several of U2's shows was "Beautiful Day" winding down with Bono's rendition of the "Sgt. Pepper's" chorus, just like he did onstage with Sir Paul during 2005's Live 8 performance. According to Jann S. Wenner in November 2005's *Rolling Stone*, Yoko Ono even called Bono "John's son" in the 1980s.

"Here's something I think you'll wanna sing along with," Paul always expressed before performing his concerts' focal point. He sat at the piano for the Beatles' best-selling single, "Hey Jude." Eight canons would explode onstage while disco lights orbited the James Bond theme, "Live and Let Die." Other ageless songs performed on 2005's expedition consisted of "Penny Lane," "Eleanor Rigby," "Good Day Sunshine," and "Back in the USSR."

Then the show's top-notch set-list would get even better. Paul stood alone to play the first verse of "Yellow Submarine," and he would jump into "I'll Follow the Sun," as well as the new record's "Follow Me." Paul often told a tale of his teenage years with George, creating the ten seconds of guitar that "became the basis" for his tour opener in 2002, "Blackbird." Midway through the White Album's masterpiece, Paul messed up the song's lyrics two different times when playing in Miami. He and the crowd simply laughed at the faux pas. "At least you know it's not on tape," Paul confessed.

On a more serious note, Bono regularly talked about his late father. He sometimes claimed that the first thing his father would say to the singer would be "Take off those fucking sunglasses," in a heavy Irish accent. Bono would then remove his eyewear and serenade his pop with "Sometimes You Can't Make It on Your Own." When in the South, he requested Spanish lessons from the crowd and sang "Love and Peace or Else." Bono tended to express that *How to Dismantle an Atomic Bomb*'s "Miracle Drug" is a song about faith, science, doctors, and nurses. The idea expressed that the twenty-first century can be full of promise.

Bono usually explained that "Sunday Bloody Sunday" no longer concerns Ireland, but it is now "about the red, white and blue. It is your song now America." The showman often declared "Miss Sarajevo" was for "the brave men and women of the United States military." Bono also regularly dedicated "Running to Stand Still," in which he played both guitar and harmonica, to the US Navy. The Edge fingered a piano, while the Bill of Rights scrolled along enormous screens above the set. During "Bullet the Blue Sky," Bono traditionally blinded himself with a bandana over his eyes. Thousands would roar at his slapstick pantomime.

He liked to tell a long story about the number being penned during the Bosnian War, when women staged a bathing suit model expo in defiance of their government. The Edge showed off his skills on a keyboard during the first verse, before the bass guitar and drums filled the room each night. "Is this the time for human rights?" Bono sang. Ropes of colored lights fell around U2's main stage and a young lady's face was displayed on the TVs. In broken English, she recited the Universal Declaration of Human Rights, discussing the abolishment of slavery and degrading punishment.

Bono and Edge, Vertigo Tour,
photo by Sean McCloskey

"Pride (In the Name of Love)," a number regularly performed in 2005, was uplifting. Thousands sang the chorus, and Bono spoke about Dr. Martin Luther King Jr. and the American dream. "Also a European Dream. An African dream," he shouted in most cities. Neon lights surrounding the stage created dozens of different nations' flags, four at a time.

Bono often raced along his platform singing "Where the Streets Have No Name," while the gray-haired Adam took a leisurely stroll around the walkway. The two would meet in the middle of the arena, where Bono threw his arms around the bass player. Yards behind the couple, the Edge could almost always be seen strutting in front of Larry. "Thank you, muchas gracias," Bono sometimes cried before requesting that the audience pull out all of their cell phones at once. The entire complexes were illuminated by mere phone receivers; quite a sight. "Twenty-first Century Woodstock," Bono labeled the spectacle at most shows.

Bono made it a point to explain that there were over two million Americans who had signed up for the campaign, entitled One, working to eradicate the world's poverty by 2008. He was proud to declare the organization's membership now exceeds that of the National Rifle Association, stretching through thirty-six countries. Bono preached about AIDS research in Africa. He concluded his sermon with the statement, "We are more powerful when we work together as one," and dove into the 1991 ballad of the same name before departing for the first time every evening.

Paul frequently took a brief encore, not allowing any fan to stop applauding or grab a refill before he reappeared. Mr. McCartney customarily presented his fans with an acoustic rendition of "Yesterday," and ordered the crowd to "get back to where" they once belonged. "Here's a song we never performed on America soil," Paul explained every night as he stole "Helter Skelter" back from U2. The band did not perform the song live on their 2004 venture. A second ridiculously quick break from the stage followed, and then Paul always ended the evenings with the mop-top Beatles' "Please Please Me," as well as 1970's "Let It Be." It came as an enormous surprise how much the early Beatles numbers, such as "I Want to Hold Your Hand," were exhilarating to their younger fans.

Like Sir Paul, U2 always took two encores. But they stretched a considerably longer length of time. During the first break, thousands of spectators roared for almost ten minutes as yellow searchlights circled the stage. At times, U2 reemerged with Bono on guitar for a slower, alternative version of "The Fly," followed by "Until the End of the World." It's no secret that some audiences were fortunate enough to hear both of the classics from *Achtung Baby* on the 2005 trek. On some occasions, the multitasking singer reappeared and shook a tambourine during *How to Dismantle*'s "All Because of You." He often lifted an adolescent to the stage to dance in the middle of "Bad." At some concerts, Bono grabbed a lucky middle-aged woman from the general-admission floor to dirty dance with on the walkway as the Edge thumbed acoustic versions of "Stuck in a Moment" and "Wild Horses." Other times, she was serenaded with the timeless "With or Without You." Bono would then kiss the lady's hand and help her down after the life-altering experience. The rock-and-roll icon clapped, bowed, and waved goodnight under a black cowboy hat.

In Denver's Pepsi Center, U2 reappeared for their second encore with the *How to Dismantle*'s "Original of the Species." Bono explained, "We've only played this once before. So if we screw up, blame the Edge." Just like the ex-Beatle, they ended their shows with material that dated back decades. Bono talked about performing the last song of the night, "40," during U2's one famous appearance in Colorado's Red Rocks. The biblical tune supplies a perfect conclusion, as Bono asks, "How long / How long *must* we sing this song." As customary on the Vertigo world tour, the evening in Denver ended with an extended drum solo, in "40." Bono shot a florescent spotlight into the crowd, creating a helicopter searchlight effect, recreating the *Rattle and Hum* cover. He would wave good-bye and make a nonchalant exit. Thousands chanted the chorus as Adam, followed by the Edge, departed the stage. Larry would finish up his extended drum solo, walk to the front of the stage, and kiss the stadium's worth of fans goodnight. The appearance of house lights always disappointed thousands who were still singing "40" in hopes of a third encore.

Many U2 fans were let down that they never heard any original material from *Rattle and Hum*, such as "Desire," the heavenly poetry of "God Part II," or the B. B. King tribute, "When Love Comes to Town." However, B. B. King did perform the single written by Bono regularly on his 2006 tour through the States.

Night after night, Paul's concerts were filled with a sublime mix of both obscure and classic material, rather than an uninspiring set-list taken exclusively from the Beatles' *1* collection or *Chaos and Creation*. Similarly, the Vertigo world tour did not revolve around either the *Best of* U2 collections or *How to Dismantle an Atomic Bomb*. They have each expressed a necessity to mix up their set-lists and cover each phase of their impressive careers. Otherwise, the fans, as well as the musicians, would grow bored by the same songs every night. Tens of millions of fans sang both the Beatles' and U2's poetry verse for verse on a nightly basis, each having special meanings to individuals. But U2 has successfully maintained the role as the greatest live band of the new millennium, even if their shows lacked the excitement of *Achtung Baby*'s Zoo TV and Bono preached too much with his political sermons. Regardless, the band continuously sells out arenas with their new singles, changes their set-lists, and even tells new stories every night, rather than merely replaying their decades-old classics matched with scripted jokes.

In the summer of 2006, thousands of North Americans were delighted to dance to Ringo and his All-Starr Band. Playing to a crowd of baby boomers, along with hundreds of their children, Ringo appeared extremely skinny in denim, sunglasses, and a beard. Kicking off with *Sgt. Pepper's* "With a Little Help from My Friends," the set-list always included Beatles classics, Latin funk, and long-haired rock from the 1980s.

Another song heard, "What Goes On" off of *Rubber Soul*, has a doo-wop feel that features the drummer's initial composing credit on a Beatles song. Ringo also liked to do the first song that he ever recorded with the other band that he used to be in, and played "Boys" off of his old crew's first album, *Please Please Me*.

Ringo performed "It Don't Come Easy," his premier solo single after the breakup of the Beatles. He also sang "Honey Don't," written by Carl Perkins, which was covered on the *Beatles for Sale* record. Ringo did the same tune at 2002's Concert for George. He often dedicated the Indian-influenced "Within You, Without You" to his best friend who passed away in 2001. Night after night, the entire audience was on its feet for the only number one single that Ringo ever sang as a Beatle, "Yellow Submarine," the evenings' obvious highlight.

Ringo would move back to his drum set in the middle of the stage and each of the All-Starrs re-created their own material. Billy Squier impressed with "Everybody Wants You." Another icon from twenty years earlier, Richard Marx, sang his upbeat and highly successful "Don't Mean Nothing" and "Should've Known Better." While both rock stars revived their decades-old careers, they appeared out of place with extremely short haircuts. It was reminiscent of David Lee Roth sporting a buzz cut while singing "Jump" on tour earlier in 2006. It just didn't work.

Edgar Winter impressed with "Free Ride," as well as his instrumental number one, "Frankenstein." Explaining the mechanism hanging from his neck, Winter stated he was the first to use "a strap-on . . . keyboard that is." Finally, Sheila E. belted out "A Love Bizarre" and performed a duet, "She's Not There," with Ringo.

He may not be the greatest singer in the business, but the "funny Beatle" certainly has a charming stage presence. Ringo's show doesn't compare to Paul's recreations of the timeless classics from the '60s, but the All-Starr Band's concerts were simply Fab.

7

Films of
a Generation

IMAGINE: JOHN LENNON is the essential documentary for collectors on DVD taken from the ex-Beatle's various home movies. Fanatics can cherish the rare and airbrushed footage put together in 1988 by director Andrew Solt. The intimate portrait of John's legacy exposes the genius behind the man. *Imagine* focuses on John's life in his own words and videos provided by Yoko Ono. The footage was taken directly from the archives of Lennon; from Liverpool to his luscious Tittenhurst Estate in Ascot, England, to the end in New York City. *Imagine* exposes all sides of the man: the angry youth, the radical, the husband, the father, the lover, the idealist, and the artist.

The *Rattle and Hum* DVD portrays U2 returning to rock and roll's roots on a pilgrimage through American blues, gospel, and rock. In 1988, the Irish band invited a forty-member film crew on the second leg of the Joshua Tree Tour in the States, and it became an enormous Hollywood affair, released in theaters. *Rattle and Hum* offers no new information to U2 fans. Director Phil Joanou's movie received massive promotion and publicity, turning many U2 fans off.

"I want to be loved and accepted by all facets of society, and not be this loud-mouth, lunatic, poet, musician. But I cannot be what I am not," Lennon expresses as the introduction to the *Imagine* documentary. The ballad "Real Love" plays over images of the English countryside running up to his Tittenhurst Estate.

Rattle and Hum starts with Bono, in his distinct brogue, stating, "This is a song Charles Manson stole from the Beatles. We're stealing it back." And U2 rips into their cover version of "Helter Skelter." In a 2006 issue of *MOJO*, the Edge discusses Paul's "heavy metal whirlpool" in his explanation of number thirty-nine of the 101 Greatest Beatles Songs. The guitarist explained, "I think we chose it because we were in this kind of helter skelter mode ourselves and it spoke to us. . . . It's so powerful and yet it maintains such a high level of melody—that's the amazing thing, to be melodic at that kind of intensity."[1] A camera flies over Ireland's green pastures, not unlike *Imagine*'s birds'-eye-view filming over Tittenhurst, while spectators listen to the Edge's vocals of "Van Diemen's Land."

Rattle and Hum is not a documentary like *Imagine*, which displays John's entire life from 1940 to 1980. As Larry explains, the U2 film is the journey of U2 going through the States in the 1980s and capturing the time period for the band. While both movies mix black-and-white photography with color shots, *Rattle and Hum*'s editing and camera work is superior. Regardless, all four members of U2 agree that the work is simply about music, just as John expresses *his* work during *Imagine*. The Beatles were about music, rather than the hype, the money, or the women.

Retracing history, *Imagine* shows John's first band, the Quarrymen. It also discusses his first meeting with Paul through a mutual friend, followed by his union with George. There is no mention in the film of the Liverpool boys being introduced to Ringo. The young crew began playing out in the rough town of Hamburg, Germany, in 1960. Fights broke out regularly, and chairs would be thrown around the room. Manager Brian Epstein talks about seeing the Beatles and getting them a record contract.

Yoko Ono had a plethora of home videos that she and John had shot of their life together, and she turned them over to the film's producers. Even if Ono had no approval or editing rights, John's wife cooperated nonetheless with the making of *Imagine*. The film moves back and forth from the early Beatles history to John at home in 1971 with his immediate family. Julian Lennon discusses growing up without his father, who was busy touring during the height of Beatlemania.

Tracing rock's American roots, the four musicians in U2 visit the historical Sun Studios in Memphis, as well as Elvis Presley's home, Graceland. Adam is interviewed while seated at a kitchen table talking straight into the camera with a cup of coffee, the same way John does in *Imagine*. Adam recalls relating to Elvis as a working man with a guitar and wanting to be that cool himself. John discusses going to watch Elvis movies as a child in Liverpool and experiencing the girls screaming at the American musician. "So I thought, that's a good job," John explained.

Imagine shows still shots of Bob Dylan. Expressing their own "belief in Zimmerman," U2 delivers a fine live version of Dylan's "All Along the Watchtower" in San Francisco. With a harmony never before associated with the poetic lyrics, Bono sings, "All I've got is a red guitar, three chords, and the truth."

Since the mid-'80s, U2 has been the king of stadium rock. The band has been entertaining in enormous arenas for years, as *Rattle and Hum* shows in multiple scenes. U2 sings "Angel of Harlem" and joins a church choir to recreate a gospel version of "I Still Haven't Found What I'm Looking For." They also perform the bluesy single "When Love Comes to Town" alongside B. B. King. "You mighty young to write such heavy lyrics," expresses the sixty-two-year-old blues legend to Bono.

The Fab Four are witty when being asked silly questions at a New York press conference in 1964. On the opposite side of the spectrum, U2 properly answers respectful questions with sincerity in their film. *Rattle and Hum* also shows the four chatting before a gig, John in his studio with Phil Spector. However, the camera displays U2 recording without disagreements or name-calling to one another or the technicians, as the impatient John does at home.

The Beatles performed a show in front of Queen Elizabeth at the Prince of Wales Theatre in London, with thousands of fans screaming during "Twist and Shout." John describes another concert in Washington, DC, as chaotic. "It was like being in the eye of a hurricane," he confesses.

Showcasing an excessive amount of information to Beatles fans, *Imagine* details why the Beatles had decided to stop touring, as listeners couldn't hear their music live with all the yelling in the audience. The film also deals with John's "bigger than Jesus" faux pas and interviews an infuriated leader of the Ku Klux Klan. The documentary shows vivid animated videos of "Strawberry Fields Forever" and "Lucy in the Sky With Diamonds." John describes his first date with Yoko, the effects of the press's harsh reaction to her, and the infamous photo of a nude John and Yoko on the cover of *Rolling Stone*, and portrays their famous "Bed-In," where the two decided to use their honeymoon as a media event for peace.

John's work was always very personal. Discussing his childhood, he talks about the tragic loss of his mother after a drunken police officer had run her over while driving his automobile. In John's ballad "Mother," he sings, "Mother, you had me but I never had you." "I am not here for you. I am here for me and her [Yoko]," John expresses in front of the camera in *Imagine*. The idea behind the ex-Beatle's blunt statement is repeated throughout the movie.

On the opposite end of the spectrum, U2 sings about the world's cultures. "Here we are, the Irish in America," Bono announces to a stadium of fans. "The Irish have been coming to America for years, going back to the great famine." The singer goes on chatting to tens of thousands about Irish immigrants and terrorism leading into "Sunday Bloody Sunday." The non-rebellious song is followed by "Pride (In the Name of Love)," a tribute to Martin Luther King Jr. "Bullet the Blue Sky" is a political number with a biblical reference: "In the locust wind comes a rattle and hum. Jacob wrestled the angel and the angel was overcome." The song also contains the familiar expression "rattle and hum."

The *Imagine* documentary is unquestionably a respectful portrait of Lennon as a musician who was extremely sincere in his work. He is shown to be a loving, gentle man who really did believe in the peace movement he perpetuated in the 1970s. In one scene, John argues bitterly with a *New York Times* journalist during his "Bed-In" for peace about his notorious nude album cover. The documentary captures John's antiwar activities, highlighted by a confrontation on a talk show hosted by conservative cartoonist Al Capp. *Imagine* is also filled with fantastic images of John as a teenager. At the same time, viewers catch extensive interviews of Yoko, John's two sons, and his first wife, Cynthia. Paul, George, and Ringo interviews are all missing from the film, despite each one appearing in earlier footage of Beatles press conferences.

Perhaps the most amazing aspect of *Imagine* is the use of John's own voice narration of the film and the incredible amount of personal footage. The authentic home videos give Beatles fans a peek into their private and public life together, as well as apart. Viewers get a glimpse of the "giving John" when they see him with a homeless transient who has been sleeping on his private estate. There is one incredibly self-indulgent scene, showing John and his wife undressing and climbing into bed together. Perhaps the most eerie moment of the film, however, is John predicting his own assassination. *Imagine* captures the Beatles' final live public appearance together, the famous rooftop performance in London where the band sings "Don't Let Me Down." Similarly, U2 once played on the roof of a rundown building in downtown Los Angeles.

The Lennon documentary draws to a conclusion with John's brutal assassination at age forty. The superbly edited footage of John's eyeglasses falling and shattering on cement in slow motion, with "A Day in the Life" playing in the background, leaves a chilling effect in the hearts of film-viewers. Of course, the newsreel footage covering the murder, followed by mourners from around the world weeping while "All You Need Is Love" plays, is not easy to digest either. Concluding *Imagine* with John idly fingering a white piano at home, the credits roll with the classic Beatles track "In My Life" playing.

Imagine paints a favorable picture of Lennon, but it does not ignore his more prominent faults in this entertaining chronicle of one of rock's greatest icons. It is far from a perfect film, with a narrative structure that jumps around without transitions. The documentary does celebrate John's world-changing art, humor, and poignancy, and the astonishing soundtrack makes *Imagine* a necessity for any Beatles fan.

In both movies, there are certain songs heard that are not included on the soundtracks. The film *Imagine* features "Come Together," "Across the Universe," and other Beatles numbers that are missing from the CD. The *Rattle and Hum* movie contains live versions of "Bad" and "With or Without You." Meanwhile, other tracks on the disc, such as the poetic "God Part II," are not present in the film.

While *Rattle and Hum* simply contains a theatrical trailer, bonus features on the *Imagine* DVD include a John Lennon Trivia Track, featuring the entire movie with extra information typed at the bottom of the screen. For example, Andrew Solt also produced the film *Willy Wonka & the Chocolate Factory* in 1971, and John was legally blind without his glasses. Then there is a shorter documentary, *John Lennon: The Music, the Memories, the Man*, with music directors and editors looking back at Lennon's influence on cultures around the world. The third feature is *John and Yoko: Truth Be Told*, a taped interview for BBC radio at the Tittenhurst Estate in 1971. John is quite candid about his music and openness to sex. He expresses the belief that there is nothing wrong with commercializing sex, comparing his own art to Shakespeare's writing. Spectators see John performing Imagine at the Apollo Theater in New York, as well as home videos of his family entertaining at their mansion in England. *The Head Master Looks Back* is a short film featuring John's old school principal, William Ernest Pobjoy, who discusses the multitalented but troublemaking John at

Quarry Bank High School in the 1950s. Finally, a trailer for a James Dean documentary closes *Imagine*'s bonus features. The DVD contains even more music and biographical information to access on the computer.

Rock Star

THE CULTURAL ICON

IMAGINE FEELING POETIC ONE NIGHT and writing a dreamy love letter to your wife. Nine months later, fifty thousand spectators sing the verses word for word. *Imagine* shaking hands with the president of the United States, getting $5 million for AIDS research, and never removing your sunglasses while doing it. *Imagine* choosing which home you shall take your kids to for the weekend—New York, Miami, Belfast, or Berlin. It's no secret Bono loves his job as the self-proclaimed last of the rock stars. In the tradition of John Lennon's humanitarian efforts, Bono has become the most successful cultural icon in Western society.

John, who would have turned sixty-seven in 2007, is as hip and as popular as ever in the twenty-first century. There is no argument that he helped make rock and roll acceptable in societies around the world. In the mid-1960s, the young man of Welsh and Irish decent became a spokesman for international causes. The Beatles rode on the postwar cultural change in Great Britain. John helped define the emerging youth of the mid-'60s through his band's type of music and its growing popularity, which defied authority, easily symbolized by long hair. The working-class lad and his mates were embraced as they attracted millions of eyes and ears to their small town of Liverpool. The English community was delighted by its sudden global attention. John's band began selling out shows in countries where few British acts had prospered, including Australia, Sweden, France, Ireland, and America.

Lennon and the Beatles' appearances on *The Ed Sullivan Show* cannot be compared to any other in television history. There has never been another TV program with the influence of Sullivan's. After all, his weekly broadcast was the "high-water mark of American mass culture," and even helped the celebrity status of Elvis Presley.[1]

The Beatles had an enormous effect on the business of transmitting music. First, Top 40 radio was growing dull in the early 1960s. After all, AM and pop radio had experienced no major trends since Elvis in the 1950s. But John and the Beatles turned that all around with hip and fresh self-penned songs from Britain. Then, prior to the Beatles' arrival, most teens had spent their disposable income on 45-rpm "singles." The Beatles' albums sold in the millions. Immediately, the electronics industry on both sides of the Atlantic experienced a sales boom as consumers required new equipment to hear the artists' increasingly complex studio work. Also, the arrival of the Beatles in 1964 soon led to the birth of serious rock journalism. The heavy and sophisticated new music could no longer be ignored, or treated as a passing fad, by the mainstream press. As news coverage increased, some folks feared that the Beatles and their music posed a cultural threat to the good old-fashioned American home with apple pie and a white picket fence. More than twenty years later, U2, fresh after releasing *The Joshua Tree*, became the fourth rock band to be featured on the cover of *Time* magazine, only after the Beatles, the Band, and the Who. And in 1967, the Beatles sang "All You Need Is Love" on the first-ever worldwide TV hookup in front of an audience estimated at four hundred million.

A quarter century after John's death, reporter Angus Batey of *MOJO* declared him as the number one music superstar: "A genius by his own reckoning . . . the ultimate rock and roll icon."[2] Meanwhile, the number seven position on that list is held by Bono, as he "makes politicians cry and Pavarotti feel humble." U2 had once fantasized of getting the ex-Beatle to produce one of their records. In fact, U2's singer once explained that he was no more than eleven years old when hearing Lennon's work blew his mind, immediately affecting his life.[3]

Picking up where the Beatle left off, Bono has been the ultimate media icon seeking planetary unity. It always seemed that he was destined to be an international superstar, as big as Lennon himself. During an interview in the early 1980s, Bono expressed, "I do feel that we are meant to be one of the great groups," and he compared the band to the Beatles, the Stones, and the Who.[4]

U2's fearless leader has spent the twenty-first century trying desperately to improve the planet. The man does everything possible to shed light on the crisis of AIDS and extreme poverty. According to Chuck Klosterman of *Spin*, "Bono is the most tangibly successful rock and roll activist of all time."[5] Not unlike John attempting to unite the 1960s and '70s civilizations to stop the Vietnam War, Bono truly believes that popular music can change the universe. In March of 2005, U2 was inducted into the Rock and Roll Hall of Fame.

Like some other great artists who died before their time, John was a preacher of love, justice, equality, integrity, and risk. He is proof that simple art can potentially alter the global state of cultures. Sean Lennon once described the scene after his father's infamous murder. According to John's son, the house had an overwhelming swarm of fans outside for several months when he was five years old.

"I look for an X-factor in music, that feeling that the musician is giving of himself," Bono once explained. "I got that from John Lennon [and] from Bob Dylan." "They didn't try to hide themselves."[6] In 1984, Bono interviewed Dylan when U2 shared the same bill as him inside Ireland's Slane Castle. The two poets discussed Dublin's music scene, the game of chess, and Dylan's legendary image of pissing people off. A few hours later, Bono joined Dylan onstage to perform "Blowin' in the Wind." The interview was immediately published in the Irish music paper *Hot Press*. "Everybody's trying to say, 'U2, the next this, the next that,'" Bono stated in 1987. "You get record industry people saying, 'As big as the Beatles.'"[7]

Not only did the Beatles get to meet their mentors, Elvis and Dylan, but they even got to play for Queen Elizabeth as well. Paul sang "Till There Was You" from the musical *The Music Man*. Prior to performing "Twist and Shout," John ordered the spectators in the less expensive seating to clap with the beat. At the same time, the rest of the audience was asked to rattle their jewelry.

Bono has also spent time with one of *his* role models, Frank Sinatra. The two celebrities were drinking whiskey just before Bono's infamous blunder at the Golden Globe Awards broadcast. U2 had won an award for Martin Scorsese's *Gangs of New York* theme song. "Fuckin' brilliant," Bono exclaimed on live television. Eventually, the FCC ruled that Bono's slip of the tongue was "fleeting" and not indecent in its context. Music reporters all over expressed suspicion that the blunder was intentional, stating that Bono simply wanted to make a gesture proving that he was not the mass media's pet by politely collecting an expected award.

There is no question that John's infamous social blunder was unintentional. On July 29, 1966, also the date of Bob Dylan's infamous motorcycle crash, *Datebook* magazine, marketing to teenage women, published an excerpt of an interview where Lennon made a blasphemous remark. "Christianity will go. It will vanish and shrink. I needn't argue with that; I'm right and I will be proved right. We're more popular than Jesus now; I don't know which will go first, rock and roll or Christianity. Jesus was alright, but his disciples were thick and ordinary. It's them twisting it that ruins it for me."[8]

The quote was reprinted out of context from Maureen Cleave's original write-up, "How Does a Beatle Live? John Lennon Lives like This," published four months earlier in London's *Evening*

Standard. The article described the Beatle's luxurious house and magnificent toys, which he frequently disregarded. American culture was immediately taken aback. Church organizations began to burn Beatles records. Of course, John made several public apologies, claiming his quote was taken out of context. Ironically, more than thirty years later, journalist John Muncie claimed John and his three mates were the most powerful forces in the history of popular music, with more influence than Elvis or even Jesus Christ.[9]

John had a love-hate affair with the press. Although some journalists crucified him, other media giants appreciated everything about him. "John Lennon was honest and straightforward and cooperative; he made me feel human right away," said *Rolling Stone* photographer Annie Leibovitz in 1971. "He made me realize we were all people and we were all here on earth." Similarly, Bono puts every reporter he meets at ease. He looks the individual straight in the eye, immediately casting honesty and affection.[10]

In the late '60s, John divorced his high school sweetheart and within one year married Yoko Ono, the daughter of a wealthy Tokyo family. The esoteric woman influenced the Beatle to be more conceptual and daring in his art and career. John and Yoko hosted numerous public appearances, including "Bed-Ins" for peace, as well as orthodox rock concerts. Perhaps the most memorable of these is the *Live Peace in Toronto* 1969 record where the famous couple was joined onstage by English guitar legend Eric Clapton. By the end of the 1960s, Yoko would not leave John's side for a moment.

In *The Beatles* (1981), McCartney shares personal statements about John to Hunter Davies in an interview. "Lennon was a maneuvering swine. Now since his death he's become Martin Luther Lennon. . . . He wasn't some sort of holy saint."[11] Of course, the media gleefully played up the statement, making Paul out to be a cynical storyteller about his legendary days with the Beatles. The "brainy Beatle" also allegedly became strung out on heroin in the mid-'70s. Meanwhile, Bono has never been divorced and his bandmates have never publicly disrespected their singer.

Several times in the 1970s, John had written songs about the other Beatles, as well as his family members. The depressing song

"Mother" depicts John's true feelings toward his natural mom, Julia Lennon, who abandoned him when he was a baby: "Mother, you had me. I never had you. I wanted you. You never wanted me." Several periodicals published in the last two month of 2004, including *Rolling Stone*, *Spin*, and *Blender*, describe U2's album *How to Dismantle an Atomic Bomb* as Bono's most personal work. Each magazine refers to the death of Bono's father in Ireland as the motivation for U2's dark album. Again, Bono is not as direct in his wording as John's autobiographical lyrics.

John also penned a number of straightforward songs about his second wife, such as "Dear Yoko": "Even after all these years, I miss you when you're not here, I wish you were here, my dear Yoko." On the other hand, Bono has usually maintained a great deal of separation between his lyrics and his personal life. On a general level, U2 songs are more abstract, allowing listeners to pull their own meanings from Bono's words. For example, rather than writing directly about his wife, Bono wrote "The Sweetest Thing," not "Sweet Ali," to convey a sincere apology for forgetting her birthday one year. The number can be found on 1998's release, *The Best of 1980–1990*.

Sean Lennon was born in 1975 and John took a hiatus from show business in order to focus on raising his second son. John had always regretted not being around when his first boy, Julian, was born to his initial wife. He published a children's book of drawings, *Real Love: The Drawings for Sean*. Several of Bono's childlike paintings and sketches are printed on the inside cover of U2's 2004 release, *How to Dismantle an Atomic Bomb*.

In the spring of 2006, Bono said that the idea of eradicating malaria, Africa's most lethal danger, in the next decade was as exciting as watching Neil Armstrong take the first walk on the moon. In fact, NBC Nightly News broadcast live from Africa one evening for the first time in history. The special report followed Bono on his trek through some of humanity's poorest nations. The trip helped earn the singer a nomination for the 2006 Nobel Peace Prize. Bono's partner in Live 8, Sir Bob Geldof, was also nominated, along with Indonesia's president and a former US Secretary

Pencil sketching, *by Daniel Camilli*

of State. Later in the year, U2 teamed up with Green Day to record punk-rock band the Skids' cover of "The Saints Are Coming." The video imagined US troops being deployed from Iraq to save Hurricane Katrina victims. Proceeds from the album sales benefited the citizens of New Orleans. Also, U2's spiritual songs, from "I Will Follow" to "Yahweh," are now being used in 260 religious congregations in seven countries. The sermons preach about everything from loving your neighbor to global poverty in both liberal and conservative churches.

Also in 2006, Yoko honored her late husband by dedicating a site in Reykjavik, Iceland, for the Imagine Peace Tower. The circular glass base supports a hundred-foot beam of light that will shine on the nation every hour of every day.

John may have lived an antiwar life of peace, but he was nonetheless brutally murdered by Mark David Chapman on December 8,

1980, outside his home in the Dakota building in New York City. John died at Roosevelt Hospital later that afternoon. Chapman is still in a New York State prison and has been denied parole numerous times over the last twenty-five years.

Lennon's singles and records were more important cultural forces in the last generation than U2's, despite MTV and the World Wide Web attracting a larger number of listeners. Lennon would have certainly been viewed on both outlets if the technology were available in his time. True, the Beatle was far from a flashy musician, but he always got the job done. On the other hand, being showy has often been part of Bono's image, whether it was playing the Fly during the Zoo TV Tour or wearing devil's horns as PopMart's Bono Macphisto.

Bono hopes to inspire listeners to think for themselves and accomplish even their toughest goals. U2's lead singer believes that there are social responsibilities that go hand in hand with being a moral celebrity. He has continually admitted he would not have a role to play if it were not for John and the Beatles.

9

Rock Star

THE POLITICAL ICON

THE BEATLES' PHENOMENAL INFLUENCE transformed their generation in many ways, from the artistic to the everyday political. As Lionel Tiger explained in *Rolling Stone*, the band's career "had been an antidote to war, living proof that societies could emerge from holocaust and horror and triumphantly reproduce."[1]

Beginning with the Toronto Peace Festival in 1969, John and Yoko performed a series of rock concerts as a statement of peace and love. After the Beatles broke up in 1970, John spent the decade working on his solo career while campaigning for world unity. He realized that his every word and move would be reported on by the press.

The same year, with the Vietnam War protest at its height, the couple held a famous press conference as their honeymoon. The pair did not leave their room in the Amsterdam Hilton for seven days. At this "Bed-In," John and Yoko gave hundreds of interviews, discussing their personal pursuit for true harmony. They talked about activism, culture, and societies at war. A few weeks later, the two staged a comparable "Lie-In" for peace in Montreal. While in Canada, they recorded an antiwar single in their hotel room with dozens of guests, including Timothy Leary, Tommy Smothers, a rabbi, a priest, and the Canadian chapter of the Radha Krishna Temple all singing backup. "Give Peace a Chance" was an enormous success for John. The song received Top 40 radio play for weeks. "Give Peace a Chance" sold a million copies worldwide, reaching number fourteen on the American charts and number two on the British charts in 1969.

Newsweek recognized "Give Peace a Chance," stating, "Now it will serve as the centerpiece for sing-ins at shopping centers planned in Washington and will join the list of carols to be sung in projected nationwide Christmas Eve demonstrations. . . . The peace movement has found an anthem."[2]

John made himself a spokesman for the fight against the war in Vietnam, bringing the Beatles into the political spotlight for the first time. At the premiere of his film How I Won the War he explained his reasons for making the movie with the strong statement, "I hate war. If there is another war I won't fight and I'll try to tell all the youngsters not to fight either. I hate all the sham." Two days later, a hundred thousand Americans marched at the Pentagon. The antiwar citizens were seeking a transformation of government policy via new forms of political expression.[3]

In the spring of 1971, thousands of veterans, organized by Vietnam Veterans against the War, rallied in Washington, DC. These men, many in wheelchairs and many missing limbs, stated their military ranks on the steps of the National Capitol. Thousands of the men were singing John's second anthem for the peace movement, "Power to the People." The song reached number eleven in the States and number six in England.

Later that year, John and Yoko moved to New York City, as the rock star was invigorated with the city's art and radical politics. The couple spent years performing at political benefits along the East Coast and appeared at social-justice events to promote an end to the war in Vietnam. They recorded a double album, Some Time in New York City, singing about drug laws, the Irish conflict, and justice for black radical Angela Davis. John and Yoko became global advocates of the nonviolent passive resistance movement that was led by Mohandas Gandhi and Martin Luther King Jr. But President Nixon saw John and Yoko as a threat to national security. In 1972, a Senate internal security subcommittee of the Judiciary Committee forwarded a memo to Senator Strom Thurmond discussing the former Beatle's political acts. It suggested that John would interfere with Nixon's renomination at the Republican Convention in San Diego. In response, it was recommended that Lennon be deported. Within weeks, he was informed that he must leave the States, based on a 1968 marijuana-possession case in England. It took years, but John and Yoko eventually had the case withdrawn. When the president was later forced to resign, Lennon told Pete Hamill in a *Rolling Stone* interview that he chose not to discuss Nixon's career. "I'm even nervous about commenting on politics," John explained. "They've got me that jumpy these days."[4]

John Lennon was a martyr, sometimes brash, but always compassionate. At the same time, he was willing to be the media's clown in order to get his point across to the public. In a 2005 issue of *Tracks* magazine, Anthony DeCurtis noted that Lennon's legacy continues to shine "on both the music scene and the culture at large." The ex-Beatle's outspokenness toward human rights was filled with "fury and love, of political righteousness and enlightened family values."[5]

During the same decade that Lennon was shot, a genuine character with no pretense rose to the public spotlight: Bono. Prior to the Irishman's discovery of the Who, the Rolling Stones, and Led Zeppelin, he recalls listening to Lennon's visions of a peaceful world. Since the release of *The Joshua Tree*, every move that Bono makes has gained a vast amount of attention. More than merely a rock star, he is looked to for his cultural and political ideas. Everything that Bono expressed to the mass media became some kind of weighty statement, as listeners took his every word to heart.

Throughout the 1980s, Bono was involved with Amnesty International, organizing fundamental and exhausting summits between superpowers for the improvement of basic human rights. He worked on the Good Friday Agreement, an arrangement intended to unite the world's differing political opinions for the common goal of everlasting peace. The agreement aimed to halt sectarian and political violence, while establishing one power-sharing executive with both unionists and nationalists sitting together in cabinet. While on the Joshua Tree Tour in 1989, Ted Mico of *Spin* reported Bono's career "must have been the nearest a rock star has ever come to being a US Presidential candidate."[6]

But Bono became turned off by governments' policies all around the world. "Politically, I'm looking around, there's elections coming up all over the place, in England, in the US I'm sick and tired of party politics. You know, the left, the right. I'm sick of the left, I'm sick of the right," he explained to *Rolling Stone*. "Even the liberals are giving me a pain in the ass. We need new solutions to new problems."[7]

Rather than giving up his frustrating career in politics, Bono kept it up with persistence, as well as a sense of humor. He impressed Bill Clinton with his wisdom, followed by George W. Bush. At many Zoo TV concerts in 1992, Bono would call a local pizzeria from his stage and order a thousand pies to go, as well as making calls to the White House. Unfortunately, the joker never reached the first President Bush on the phone, but audiences loved when he flirted with an Oval Office operator. Years prior, Bono told Chuck Klosterman of *Spin* that "the problem with voting is that no matter who you vote for, the government always gets in."[8]

Before entering the new millennium, Bono and the Edge joined two Irish politicians, Ulster Unionist leader David Trimble and his counterpart in the nationalist Social Democratic and Labour Party, John Hume, at a campaign concert to show unity in Northern Ireland. Onstage, they all performed renditions of the Beatles' "Don't Let Me Down," "Give Peace a Chance," and "One."

Bono considers himself a socialist. His father was from the working class and the singer grew up in a blue-collar home. Today, Bono is more aggressive when it comes to politics. Experiencing the famine in Africa, as well as having children of his own, has made the man insistent about improving living conditions all around the world. He has been pelting the media and the politicians who run the arms of America. Regardless of his persuading actions and lectures, Bono never tries to convince anyone to back either Republicans or Democrats. "Our audiences are very smart, and if I abuse that relationship it would simply end," he said in the year 2000. "If I told people how to vote, they would tell me, 'Go fuck yourself.'"[9]

In 2002, Josh Tyrangiel of *Time* magazine wrote, "Like Superman turning into Clark Kent, the earnest politician operative took over." Bono's straightforward remarks and global fame earned him political cache in the eyes of the public.[10] The rock star told Tyrangiel that he has given up on music as a political force. But Bono certainly changed his mind in the few years that followed, as he has been continuously involved with the White House. "I'll never forget one day during my Administration," explained Bill Clinton, "Secretary [Lawrence] Summers comes in and says, 'You know. Some guy just came in to see me in jeans and a T-shirt, and he just had one name, but he sure was smart.'"[11] Bono sat with New York Mayor Michael Bloomberg and Clinton at the 2004 Democratic Convention.

Bono spent a good part of that year touring Africa, focusing attention on poverty and diseases, such as AIDS. He also sat with the World Economic Forum with Microsoft giant, Bill Gates. Bono met with George W. Bush at the Inter-American Development Bank. While everyone else was complaining about Bush, Bono persuaded the president to give a billion dollars for Africa. He later told *Q* magazine's Paul Rees that he would "have lunch with the devil to secure a donation" for Africa, even after the Edge begged Bono not to meet the president. But the lead singer has great judgment. He is bipartisan and the end justifies the means.[12]

In March of 2005, Bono was named as a potential, but unlikely, candidate to lead the World Bank. It would have been rare to see an Irishman on an American board. He also held a meeting with President Bush on the famine in Africa at the G8 Summit in Scotland. Bono helped make world leaders commit an unprecedented investment of $50 billion per year in lifesaving assistance by 2010. Most people around the world know Bono as a rock star, but he understands what it takes to get voters' attention to raise money and earn beneficial results for mankind.

At a concert in Vancouver in the spring of 2005, Bono requested that 18,000 spectators phone Canadian politician Paul Martin and ask him to raise the amount of the country's foreign aid. The man realizes just how much celebrities in the entertainment industry and politicians have in common. They all perform for people's satisfaction with a sense of occasion. James Traub of the *New York Times* reported, "Bono somehow manages to be righteous without being self-righteous. I suppose because he understands that it's not about himself."[13]

The recording rights to *Imagine*, as well as John's entire solo songbook, were used to harness the power of music. Yoko gave the entire catalog away as a gift to Amnesty International in order to inspire a new generation to celebrate and stand up for human rights, just one of Bono's many campaigns. In 2005 alone, big-name pop artists, including the Cure, Snow Patrol, Duran Duran, and the Black Eyed Peas, covered Lennon material. Every couple of months the Amnesty International released four covers of John's songs to buy via its Web site, with the proceeds benefiting those less fortunate. U2 also won Amnesty's 2005 Ambassador of Conscience Award for their continuing commitment to equality. By the end of the year, Bono joined Mr. and Mrs. Bill Gates as one of *Time* magazine's prestigious People of the Year, a result of his ongoing charitable acts.

In the year 2006, Bono met with Bush again on presidential jet Air Force One to discuss AIDS. Bono's charity efforts earned him a distinct Lego Burning Man statue at a German ceremony in January. There are literally "millions he manages to touch everyday with his music and his heart," wrote Jesse Helms, former Senator and conservative from North Carolina, in *Time*'s Heroes & Pioneers; he was also listed in the Artists & Entertainers listing of the hundred most influential people of 2006.[14]

In the twenty-first century, Bono is the most successful political figure in popular culture. He has marketed himself to the entire world, making more dollars for just causes than Lennon ever achieved. The Beatles would have experienced some type of mediocre sales if the four had lasted a quarter century. But a U2 anthology will not be selling by the millions in forty years. Bono is the better icon. The Irishman is a more successful politician, campaigning on global debt issues and human rights. It's no secret that the Fly cannot compare to the Walrus when it comes to music. Nothing can. U2's harmonies and melodies do not equal the Beatles' catalog. Nothing ever will in terms of a cultural revolution. But as a political icon, as a godly poet, as a performer, and as a role model for children, Bono is the soaring voice, the ultimate celebrity who outshines John Lennon.

For decades, Bono has been spinning in the revolution that the Beatles created, not watching it go 'round. It's been over twenty-five years, entailing Live Aid in 1985, Amnesty International's "Conspiracy of Hope" tour in 1986, and 2005's Live 8, and the high-paying public is not sick of U2. As much as Bono enjoys his work campaigning as an activist, he accepts that his primary job is as a rock star.

10

The Tribute
Bands

IN THE 1970S, mainstream rock moved out of intimate club settings and into arenas, as imitation acts moved to restaurants and bars. Commonly covered groups include Black Sabbath, Led Zeppelin, AC/DC, and the Grateful Dead. While most imitation bands begin in order to push an original outfit, other cover crews play for easy money, which most music lovers hate to see. Some of these troupes are better than others. Perhaps the most widely covered ensemble ever is the Beatles, while "Yesterday" is often called the most covered song in history. There are several Beatles cover bands that attempt to re-create the look and the feel of the group by wearing the wigs and full costumes. They try to play the music note-for-note. Although these Beatles cover bands may be fun to watch, observers feel that Hello Goodbye possesses more of a Beatles-like energy onstage than the others. Spectators want to experience what it was actually like to see the originals in a living, breathing environment, and Hello Goodbye is happy to oblige.

In America, a compulsory license allows a band to sing onstage a previously recorded song without getting the permission of the copyright holder. A group of musicians can then regularly perform imitations of popular songs. However, in order to record another band's material, the new artists would have to pay licensing fees to the copyright holders. Otherwise, the music will not be legal.

One act, 1964, The Tribute, a gang out of South Carolina, ranked 167 out of the Top 200 box-office grossing bands for 2004. The cover band has played over three thousand live gigs in the last twenty-five years. Both Backbeat from Ohio and Fabmania out of Delaware tour the nation. Chicago is home to two different bands: American English and British Export. Austin, Texas features the Eggmen. The Sun Kings hail from Alameda, while the Fab Four performs in California as well. Australians can experience the Fabfour, while the Fab 4 plays shows in Switzerland. The United Kingdom is home to Beatles tribute bands, such as the Fake Beatles, the Backbeat Beatles, and the Upbeat Beatles. Liverpool Legends is managed by Louise Harrison, sister of the late George.

Perhaps the strangest of the cover acts is Beatallica. Formed in Milwaukee, the act combines the harmonies and costuming of the Beatles with the hyper-speed of Metallica. Beatallica dresses like the British in Sgt. Pepper uniforms but possesses the screaming guitar and banging drums of the American heavy metal giants. They released two parody albums, *A Garage Dayz Nite* and *The Grey Album*. Both are free to download on the band's Web site but cannot be sold until clearance is obtained from Sony/ATV Music, which owns the rights to most of the Beatles' catalog. In 2005, Beatallica were served with a cease-and-desist order for willful copyright infringement. But the site went back online after ten thousand fans signed an online petition for Sony to get off of Beatallica's back.

Hello Goodbye is a tribute act in South Florida that stays busy keeping the joy of the Beatles' music alive each week. After performing throughout the area, Hello Goodbye has successfully connected with a small, yet firm, fan base. Hearing them and seeing them in the venue they're in, fans of the Beatles love the energy that Hello Goodbye emits at each of its shows. "We try to show the crowd what it might have been like to actually see the Beatles live, as opposed to listening to the *Anthology* a million times," said guitarist Joe Bonilla.

Spreading the message of peace for a few hours, unlike today's musical age of personal prestige and gangsta rap, is appropriate at this terrorizing point in time. Every Saturday, hundreds get to experience Hello Goodbye having nothing but fun during each of their sets, conveying the idea of pure love and harmony that never ages.

Hello Goodbye enjoys playing in English pubs because they get to perform for such a lovely crowd of jokers and smokers, ranging in age from their thirties to sixties. Occasionally, they get younger spectators, who blend into the scene. By virtue of mere music, many generations come together on Hello Goodbye's dance floor for dozens of Beatles songs during any of their three-set evenings.

Dressed all in black, Hello Goodbye sometimes opens with "A Hard Day's Night." After "Ticket to Ride" is played, listeners clap and sway their hips to the Beatles' release "Love Me Do." Conceivably the greatest part of a Hello Goodbye show is hearing unfamiliar tracks, as there are many unsung Beatles classics, such as "I'll Cry Instead" and the bluesy "Baby's in Black."

Waiting for the band to sing the track "Hello, Goodbye," the room usually gets packed with over one hundred bar-goers dancing to the familiar "Sgt. Pepper's." The boys harmonize a slow version of "Norwegian Wood" with a little help from the audience, and the guitar gently weeps during "You've Got to Hide Your Love Away." One of the highlights every evening is sure to be "Twist and Shout," followed by "Hey Jude." There is usually fantastic inter-play between the four musicians, as they all bounce around like the Beatles.

Some Beatles favorites are saved until the third set, when spectators get to experience "All You Need Is Love," "Rocky Raccoon," and "Revolution." Hello Goodbye takes the room on a "Magical Mystery Tour" and sings about how lucky they are "Back in the USSR." Blair King Jr., the drummer from Philly, smiles from ear to ear behind a pair of shades and a set of percussions with a psychedelic woman painted on the outside.

Hello Goodbye usually concludes its evenings with "The End," leading into "Dizzy Miss Lizzy," and into the number "Rock & Roll Music." Until these birds have flown, Hello Goodbye shows, as well as most Beatles cover bands' performances, are almost always exciting and inviting. Music lovers from every walk of life can see the fab time these bands have onstage, possessing and caressing their audiences, night after night. Check into a Beatles cover act by you. You'll dig it.

U2's beautiful ways are currently mimicked by over forty tribute bands in the States alone. Each of the musicians dresses the part, while utilizing equivalent instruments, props, and lighting as the Irishmen. The original four embrace the attention. In the ongoing quest for authenticity, the passionate acts pay homage to U2, reenacting singles that date back to 1979. Set-lists regularly include popular favorites as well as unsung material. Even Better

UV's Angelico Mysterioso,
photo by Todd McFliker

Than the Real Thing is a group that stems from New Zealand, and An Cat Dubh is from Italy. There's a British crew who call themselves Elevation. Similarly, a cover band from Chicago possesses the same name. The Unforgettable Fire, based out of New York, once played a special St. Patrick's performance in Times Square, and the Big Apple's 2U appears all around the globe.

Touring internationally for years, 2U plays more shows in a year than

Hello Goodbye, *photo by Todd McFliker*

U2, as they headline Irish pubs, colleges, festivals, glitzy night-clubs, and charity events. Some of the crew's most memorable venues include Manhattan's Hard Rock Café and B. B. King Blues Club, on top of Penn State University, where Bono made a historical speech during the 2002 graduation ceremony. In Mexico, 2U played four shows in five days, along with European dates in 2006. The following year, they will entertain in Dublin for St. Patty's Day, as well as for the festive twenty-fifth anniversary of Red Rocks in June of 2008.

For decades, U2's anthems have been keeping musicians around the world off of troubled streets, pushing their artistic boundaries with pure integrity, while providing the phenomenal experiences of playing the role of the world's most recognized rock group. "The songs are so well crafted that they stand the test of time, regardless of who is recreating the material," said Vincent Tattanelli, drummer of 2U.

Centered in Fort Lauderdale, UV re-creates U2's unmistakable sounds and look onstage. Draped in a familiar black hat, leather jacket, a T-shirt, and jeans, front man Angelico Mysterioso plays the role of the politician behind sunglasses. Opening with "City of Blinding Lights," audiences around North America witness replications ranging from U2's first single, "Out of Control," to their 2004 radio hit "Vertigo." Couples slow dance to the melodic "All I

Want Is You" and *The Joshua Tree*'s timeless "Where the Streets Have No Name." Top 40 material performed almost always includes "Sunday Bloody Sunday," "The Fly," and "Beautiful Day." Less popular tunes consist of "Angel of Harlem" with Angelico's uplifting harmonica, before he steals back "Helter Skelter."

During "Bullet the Blue Sky," the singer often shoots a beam of light at the audience as well as at the guitarist in a woolly cap, Eddie Steklasa. The silhouette created resembles the cover to *Rattle and Hum*. Edgy Eddie steps up for "Until the End of the World," as Angelico dances in the background, hopping up and down. He then sways on his knees, singing about "Love, Love surrounding" him and "going down" on him. The evening's highlight always consists of "Mysterious Ways," when an accomplished belly dancer parades around the stage, not unlike U2's memorable video. Sandy, the exotic mistress, drapes herself in green and gold, showing off her belly button rings.

"We are trying to impersonate U2 as authentically as possible. There are some trademark moments that people know and I want to make sure we're faithful to the real thing," said Angelico. The members of UV are preparing to tour internationally, pelting men, women, and children with their U2 presentation.

Growing up on the classics, like the Beatles, Hendrix, and Zeppelin, each of the tribute acts can compare U2 performances to a religious experience. The ultimate rock stars' repertoire makes a living for the musicians as they travel the world and play what they love. Meanwhile, each performer has tremendous respect for Bono.

"I want to do the music justice, but I also want people to think they are watching the four lads from Dublin, themselves," said Eddie. "If the audience members walk away thinking they just saw and heard the real deal, or at least the next best thing, we've done our job." According to the members of UV, U2 stands as the Beatles of the current generation's culture. In fact, Blair King Jr. bangs percussion for UV as well as Hello Goodbye.

Blair contends that *Meet the Beatles!* was the very first record that he ever practiced and learned, as the music touched him. The

UV's Angelico Mysterioso, *photo by Todd McFliker*

English tunes, in addition to many other great repertoires, became the soundtrack to the drummer's life. Despite the bedlam that followed the Beatles, Blair has always gravitated to artists that find more than their personal artistic arena to express themselves in, such as Lennon, Joni Mitchell, and Bono.

Upon discovering U2 and their vigor in the 1980s, "I thought it sounded a little like fitting a square peg into a round hole," Blair explained. "It was full of youthful energy, but lacked the musicianship that I had come to admire and respect." Everything changed in the early 1990s with *Achtung Baby*. Blair knew instinctively that U2 was the band of his generation.

"When I saw U2 on the Vertigo tour in 2004," he continued, "I was struck by how much the crowd was similar to what I would expect a Beatle concert would be like without all of the exaggerated mania that accompanied the performances.

"Whether my band is re-creating the Beatles or U2, I refuse to accept that these are just *words, poetry,* or *songs,*" Blair continued. "I believe that they are extensions of what we already know, such as respect one another and the equality of man. At any rate, I feel as though U2 are the Beatles of this generation in that they are trying to make sense of, and effect, change in a confounding environment and social climate. Personally, I get to pass along the peaceful messages inherent in the two acts' music. And for that reason alone, I am blessed.

"Both acts spoke or speak of higher ideals for all of us," Blair continues. "I perform the music as a means of helping to spread the messages that both these repertoires represent. I firmly believe that all human beings can all get along together and that we can overcome our distinct differences. We can come *together* as *one* spirit of humanitarianism and equality for all genders, races, creeds, and tribes."

11

The Beatles and U2 for Sale

Twenty years after Michael Jackson outbid Paul McCartney for the rights to 251 Beatles classics, Jackson has agreed to sell his 50 percent holdings in the Sony/ATV publishing company. The catalog is worth an estimated $1 billion. Perhaps Paul will purchase back some of his band's original material. After all, he became the richest man in England during the mid-'90s, thanks to the sales of *The Beatles Anthology* compact discs and its video feature.

The *Anthology* documentary was the surviving group members' own version of their history, with hundreds of clips taken from their personal archives ranging from the British Invasion to personal chat sessions in the 1990s. In December 1993, George Martin announced that the release would be accompanied by eight CDs and a group-authorized book history. Paul, George, and Ringo each taped interviews separately, and Martin combed through some four hundred hours of Beatles outtakes and other rare audio documents. Yoko was asked if her late husband had left any solo recordings that the Beatles could use as overdubs, and in January 1994 she presented "the Threetles" with four unfinished demos, "Free as a Bird," "Real Love," "Grow Old with Me," and "Now and Then." "We just imagined John had gone on holiday and had said to us, 'Finish them up, lads—I trust you,'" Paul explained.[1]

Anthology begins with a short cut from Marlon Brando's film *The Wild One*. There is a rough motorcycle gang in the film who label themselves "The Beetles." While the classic film may have influenced the band's name, the British Board of Film Censors banned the movie in England until 1968. As a result, the likelihood of the four having knowledge of *The Wild One* during the late 1950s and early '60s is questionable.

Interesting tales explained in the documentary include all four icons discussing their families, childhoods, and discovery of musical instruments. One example is how Paul talked down to George when they were in grade school, as McCartney was older. Paul discusses seeing John for the very first time and being asked to join the Quarrymen. The boys' first-ever recording, "That'll Be the Day," is discussed, as well as heard, on both the film and its soundtrack. The recording of *Sgt. Pepper's* is examined, along with the obstacle of wives becoming involved in the band's business. *The Beatles Anthology* is a must-have for any fan, as it tracks the band through the 1960s and afterwards, telling personal stories that were completely unheard of prior to the release of the video.

In April 2006, rock antique collectors in London had the opportunity to grab a John Lennon school exercise book entitled *My Anthology*. The journal from 1952 contains a drawing of the Walrus, later seen in 1967's *Magical Mystery Tour* movie. John's book was sold off for an estimated hundred thousand pounds. The sale also included large collections of remarkable artifacts once belonging to the other Beatles and U2 members.

In 1997, an English symphony teamed up with the London Pop Choir to record an album of Fab covers, titled *The London Symphony Orchestra Plays the Music of the Beatles* (Symphonic Rock Series). The fourteen famous tracks include psychedelic tunes, such as "Strawberry Fields Forever," ballads "Yesterday" and "Let It Be," and radio favorites "Sgt. Pepper's Lonely Hearts Club Band" and "All You Need Is Love." Eight years later, various artists put together *The Greatest Hits of the Beatles: Classical Style*. Again, listeners can enjoy an eclectic mix of Beatles tunes, ranging from Ringo's light-hearted "Yellow Submarine" to the best-selling "Hey Jude."

Along the same lines as the concerto pop tunes, *The Royal Philharmonic Orchestra Plays the Music of U2* was released in 1999. The album is one disappointing orchestral arrangement after another. It lacks the emotion of the real artists, while the material is lackluster and unoriginal. Never before could listeners imagine U2's best numbers being used as elevator music.

A dozen of U2's popular singles have also been recorded by a string quartet on an album from the year 2000, properly titled *Strung Out On U2*. The talented musicians are truly worth a listen, as some singles, such as "Where the Streets Have No Names," "Mysterious Ways," and "The Sweetest Thing," cross over surprisingly well. However, a few songs, such as the Section's rendition of "Bad" and "Desire" by the Savitri String Quartet, are simply painful for U2 fans to listen to.

Another collection of the group's hits is captured on 2001's *Pickin' on U2*, an album of bluegrass instrumental renditions. The album ranges from folk to blues, as well as roots rock, gospel, and country, not unlike the Irishmen themselves. The crafted counterplay of a five-string banjo, mandolin, fiddle, and slide guitar replacing Bono's lyrics pays an impressive homage to U2's politically charged anthems "Pride (In the Name of Love)" and uplifting favorites such as "Mysterious Ways." Two years later, a more diversified compilation was put together for *Pickin' on U2, Vol. 2*. The second release offers an improvisational western feel in its ten tracks, as it contains a broader range of the band's career. Highlights include "Sunday Bloody Sunday," "Even Better than the Real Thing," and, of course, the exquisite "Beautiful Day."

Paul made a few bucks after his tour by putting out *Back in the US Live 2002*. The double CD is made up of thirty-five familiar favorites from his sold-out US tour, along with a thirty-two-page collector's booklet of photos. Two-thirds of the career retrospective tracks stem from the Beatles broad catalog, along with Paul's solo work, including "Jet," "Maybe I'm Amazed," "Band on the Run," and a number about September 11, "Freedom." Unquestionable high points consist of "Hey Jude," "Eleanor Rigby," and "I Saw Her Standing There."

The sound captured, including thousands of screaming Beatles fans, is extraordinary. Somewhat disappointing, however, is that all of the musicians' chitchat between the songs has been edited out. Listeners can feel the missing conversation, mainly song histories and band member introductions, especially when Paul sings a tribute to John, "Here Today," and "Something" to his recently departed mate, George.

Almost annually, the Beatles' drummer has teamed up with various celebrities of the industry to create the All-Starr Band. While the old crew included Peter Frampton, Jack Bruce, and Gary Brooker, the new millennium's lineup has consisted of Shelia E., Colin Hay, and other pop stars from the '80s and '90s. The All-Starr Band continuously hits the road and puts out live albums, including 2004's release, *Tour 2003*. For the most part, consumers spend their dough on Ringo's bandmates as much as the famous musician from Liverpool.

It's always fun to hear any versions of Beatles tunes led by Ringo, such as "With a Little Help from My Friends," "Don't Pass Me By," and "Yellow Submarine." Onstage, the band also performs a memorable tribute to George, an acoustic version of "Here Comes the Sun," though it is missing from the album. The material sung by the talented Shelia E. is the highlight of *Tour 2003*; the diva steals the show. Colin Hay of the 1980s' Men at Work sings a couple of tunes, including an exciting version of "Who Can It Be Now." John Waite performs two pieces that were enormously successful in their day but have not aged well. Similarly, Paul Carrack executes an unimpressive "Living Years." Though some of the tracks are amusing, *Tour 2003* is uninspiring; the cut lacks the thrilling power of the All-Starr Band's concert performances.

Hitting the market in 2004, John Lennon's *Acoustic* is pure beauty; the former Beatle's music is stripped to its raw essence. Since John never actually got around to releasing a complete acoustic collection, his wife, Yoko Ono, has taken on the task of offering the public seventeen John originals, including two live performances in 1971, one in Ann Arbor and the other at the Apollo theater. Though many of these tracks had been previously available on 1998's *Anthology: John Lennon* box set, the CD includes seven previously unreleased selections. *Acoustic* comes with a booklet that includes John's lyrics, tablature, and chord diagrams. There is a memorable quote from the ex-Beatle under a photograph of John and his son, Sean, on the inside cover: "A dream you dream you dream alone is only a dream. A dream you dream together is reality."

The title of the first track, "Working Class Hero," is sarcastic, as opposed to narcissistic. It is a self-portrait of a cynical John. He explains that his dreams have come true, but he has realized that his dreams were merely illusions. In the song, John also criticizes societies' classes, as well the media, for commercializing sexuality and drugs. The acoustic strumming will remind listeners of an essential Beatles role model, Bob Dylan. Unfortunately, "Working Class Hero" never grew into an anthem for the middle class across the world.

The opening number on U2's 2004 release, *How to Dismantle an Atomic Bomb*, as well as its initial radio single, is "Vertigo." The Spanish lyrics are numbers out of order, "Uno, dos, tres, catorce." The wordplay, one, two, three, fourteen, may be a passionate reference to the band's fourteenth album, as they have twelve from the studio and two live releases. The first verse discusses one's soul fighting with his conscience over the right thing to do, as opposed to what would be more fun. The Edge's spunky guitar tone gives off a garage rock feel throughout the piece. In the bridge, Bono sings, "All of this can be yours." The expression is a close paraphrase of Matthew 4:9, when Christ is being tempted by Satan in the wilderness. The number concludes with a message: love is the answer to understanding and enjoying the world. The first song on *How to Dismantle* is the album's best.

Meanwhile, the greatest gem on the Lennon CD, "Watching the Wheels," is surprisingly tender as an acoustic demo. The sound is even more poignant here than on the polished single. In "Watching the Wheels," John merely explains his five-year hiatus from the merry-go-round of the public spotlight, from 1975 to 1980. The lyrics express questions he would often hear, including "Surely you're not happy now, you no longer play the game," and "Don't you miss the big time boy?" John offers the subtle reply, "I'm just sitting here watching the wheels go round and round," and he was happy to do exactly that.

Bono conveys deep messages about faith, life, and death in "Miracle Drug." It was written about one of Bono's classmates who was a paraplegic. Eventually, doctors were able to attach an extraordinary device to his head that allowed him to type, and the student wrote an inspiring collection of poems. Again, Bono quotes the Holy Book as he links the mission of science and medicine with God's work with certainty.

John's "Look at Me" revolves around a lover's lack of confidence. It was performed here on guitar, as opposed to piano. The song's origins date back to 1968. It is filled with warmth, tempered by John's confessions of deep uncertainty. "Look at Me" was written when John was in the process of leaving his first wife for Yoko, and tells the story of a mortal man who acknowledges that his only true existence is in the eyes of his partner.

John's duty was always to give more affection. "Love" is a gorgeous alternate version of the song off of John's first solo album. The tender ballad consists of an uncomplicated, but exquisite, piano line. John once referred to the song as a composition he considers as memorable as anything ever recorded with the Beatles. "Real Love" is undoubtedly one of the most touching singles on *Acoustic*. John gently sings about "All the little boys and girls living in this crazy world" who are left alone. He explains that their solitude comes about despite all of the people's "plans and schemes."[2] Unfortunately, that is real life.

In cursing his own drinking due to separation anxiety from Yoko, John wrote "What You Got." The number consists of a repetitive catch phrase, "You don't know what you got, until you lose it." Even if John did not intend on being a drag, "What You Got" does not stand up to the other numbers on *Acoustic*. "Dear

Yoko" was written while John was miles away at work and missing his wife terribly. Despite its simple beauty, the song suffers from a consistent fuzzy tape noise that the record studio's sound engineers could not remove. Mixed with a jangling piano and wheezy harmonica, its straightforward message of pure love still shines through.

Dealing with a different type of relationship's hardship, "I'm a Man," Lennon's Bo Diddley cover, is about a shameless romance. Either a gentleman or a lady is head over heels for another but is forced to keep the feelings under wraps. There is a constant fear present of unreturned feelings and a friendship crushed. During *Atomic Bomb*'s "Man and a Woman," Bono sings, "For love and faith and sex and fear." It sounds as if the subject doesn't want to chance losing the love of his or her life by exposing the true feelings for the other person.

It comes as no surprise that Yoko influenced her husband to write the feminist song "Woman Is the Nigger of the World." She would often take a stand to John, pointing out little sexist behaviors in their everyday lives, such as the man reading the newspaper every morning before she did. John acknowledged that she was the first woman to demand parity with him. It contains vivid lyrics, sharp opinions, and some unfamiliar ideas in the mainstream culture. Yet the most difficult part of listening to the acoustic number is the use of the word "nigger," rather than its feminist content. John defines the word as someone whose lifestyle is defined by others, rather than a person of African descent.

There is a clenched, grunge-like guitar in John's "Well Well Well," but the acoustic version is neither new nor special to fans. The rippling piano introduction of "God" interlocking with distinguished chords is extraordinary. It is John's explicit exposition of his outlook of the world in 1970, just two months before the Beatles officially broke up. "God" is an attempt for John to counsel all Beatles fans to accept his work as a solo artist, and the number is quite memorable, even if the *Acoustic* version is a drop in sound recording quality compared to Lennon's *Anthology* edition.

U2's "Yahweh" is, of course, named after the biblical Hebrew God. It is a powerful track about the band's Christian faith in which Bono expresses humbling oneself to get into Heaven. Men and women must give up everything to God. It was written with poetic metaphors, allowing listeners to interpret the messages on different levels regardless of denomination. Some may hear lyrics about the Middle East, while other listeners may interpret "Yahweh" as Bono's personal prayer for the world. Bono sounds humble and sincere, without expressing the shallow cynicism behind the things he doesn't believe in.

Discussing God again, U2's "Love and Peace or Else" represents one laying down his sins to Yahweh, along with the state of the world. While singing, Bono prays for people with the hope of them living long and happy lives. He is searching for peace and pleads to them to put down their weapons, specifically in the Middle East. In the nature of Lennon in his later years, Bono requests that they live their entire lives and live them peacefully.

The nursery-rhyme melody of Lennon's "My Mummy's Dead" explains John's pain of never knowing his mother on a personal level. The simple and straightforward lyrics are enough to put a lump in any listener's throat. Similarly, the highly emotional "Sometimes You Can't Make It on Your Own" is a loving tribute to Bono's dad, who had recently passed away of cancer. There is a lovely crescendo near the ending of the confessional ballad where the three U2 instruments explode in a magnificent eruption. *How to Dismantle* also features "One Step Closer," a song about death. The singer isn't sure what awaits him, but he feels that everything in his life is slipping away. Yet, each step toward the end brings him one step closer to knowing the answers he can't find within himself. The lyrics were obviously invoked from the death of Bono's father as well, along with the deceased man's confusion over his faith. Now that he has passed, he will finally figure out the necessary solutions to swing his decision one way or the other.

Illegal drugs have often been synonymous with rock-and-roll stars. Yet the subject was rarely addressed in popular music thirty-five years ago. When John and Yoko decided to have a child in August 1969, John was determined to quit using heroin as an artistic indulgence. Although John's son inspired him to quit using drugs cold turkey, U2's "Original of the Species" is a highly emotional tune about the Edge's daughter. Not unlike John's lament, the U2 song was obviously written and performed with plenty of emotion. The beginning of the number, "Baby slow down," describes parents' feelings when they realize that a child has grown up and gained independence. They think that time has gone by too quickly, as if their child has been running somewhere and needs to slow down.

Being a liberal pacifist, John originally recorded a folk song, "Luck of the Irish," on his 1971 record *Some Time in New York City*. In the live version of the number, Yoko lends her husband a hand by performing in a faux Irish accent. John was always proud of his Irish heritage and often referred to Liverpool as "the capital of Ireland." At the end of "Luck of the Irish," John offers the crowd some reassurance to world peace: "So flower power didn't work, so what, we'll start over."

U2 sings "City of Blinding Lights," a number about New York City. In the lyrics "They're advertising in the skies / For people like us," Bono references the less-fortunate citizens in poor countries who are subject to advertisements for products they can never afford. Sticking to the same theme, "All Because of You" is U2's muscular single about the people of New York City and their rebirth after 2001's tragic episode of terror. There is an image of the big city life, both physically and metaphorically, with "Squashed crossing the tracks / High rises on their backs" representing tall buildings that residents work in. The line "I'm not broke but you can see the cracks" represents breaks in the sidewalks and a general decay of the unique city.

John Sinclair was a left-wing activist author and beat poet of the American '60s counterculture who received a brutal ten-year jail sentence for passing two joints to an undercover narcotics agent in 1970. Lennon wrote "John Sinclair" as a protest song against Sinclair's sentence. The live version on *Acoustic* maintains pungent lyrics but lacks elegance.

Rather than protesting the government, *How to Dismantle*'s "Crumbs from Your Table" seeks support. Reminiscent of "I Still

Haven't Found What I'm Looking For," it begins as a simplistic cry but transforms into a complex ballad concerned with Africa's hunger, debt, and fight against AIDS: "Where you live should not decide, Whether you live or die." The final verse states U2's moral-building mission, to better the world with unity.

Lennon's *Acoustic* includes a touching version of "Imagine," recorded live. Perhaps the most widely revered of all of John's singles, "Imagine" was ranked number three in *Rolling Stone*'s "500 Greatest Songs of All Time." The churchlike tenor was written in John's English estate in 1971, and the serene piece is touched by the elementary beauty of graceful piano chords. "Imagine" is a sincere statement in John's quest for world peace that has its origins in Yoko's book of poetry, *Grapefruit*, published in 1964. One of Yoko's rhythms reads, "Imagine one thousand suns in the sky at the same time . . ." Another poem begins with, "Imagine your body spreading rapidly all over the world like a thin tissue . . . ," and a third piece tells readers to "Imagine the clouds dripping." *Acoustic* concludes with a minute-long instrumental entitled "It's Real."

Although the sound quality is at times raw, the material is poetic, and the tracks have a way of growing on listeners with each time the CD is heard. *Acoustic* is melodic, and the songs are home-spun. Indeed, John would have flourished in the "unplugged" era. On the other hand, many U2 fans are disappointed in *How to Dismantle an Atomic Bomb*, as many of the pop tunes are colorless. It lacks timeless material. Despite containing all new songs, listeners come across nothing fresh from the band, as they offer no experimentation, re-creation, or even creation. In fact, the 2004 release is the first U2 album that consciously emulates its predecessor.

Released in September 2005, at the time of his global tour, *Chaos and Creation in the Backyard* finds Sir Paul in a tastefully restrained form. At the recommendation of George Martin, the album was produced by the creative Nigel Godrich, of Radiohead fame. Poignant numbers, such as "Riding to Vanity Fair," contain haunting chimes and heartfelt lyrics, matched with Beatles-like multitracked vocals. "Jenny Wren" and "Anyway" are great examples of McCartney's extraordinary gift for tender tunes, yet the simplistic rhymes and feel-good uppers manage to steer clear of cheesy pop numbers reminiscent of Wings.

Chaos and Creation is one of Paul's finest achievements, with great depth lyrically and an introspective tone. The versatile artist provides almost all the instrumentation himself on the guitar, piano, bass, and percussion. As a direct result, the record displays Sir Paul's full range of matchless talents. The album earned McCartney five Grammy nominations in 2005, including Album of the Year.

Before Live Aid, hunger-ridden Bangladesh became a disaster zone after a cyclone wiped out three hundred thousand residents. Indian sitar master Ravi Shankar planned a benefit concert with a little help from his friend George Harrison. In a matter of weeks, the former Beatle organized the first-ever trendsetting, rock star–studded charity event, *The Concert for Bangladesh—George Harrison and Friends* in Madison Square Garden on August 1, 1971.

The two-disc Grammy-winning DVD was shot on 16mm by Saul Swimmer. Following a quick interview of George at *Concert for Bangladesh*'s press conference, the show kicks off with serious Indian music, setting the mood in New York. George's set entails selections from his solo work and the number written for the event, "Bangladesh." He also sings a few Fab classics never before heard live, including "Here Comes the Sun" and "Something." George exchanges impressive solos with Eric Clapton during "While My Guitar Gently Weeps." Bob Dylan, who hadn't played live in five years, performs "A Hard Rain's A-Gonna Fall," "Blowin' in the Wind," and "Just Like a Woman." Billy Preston sings the extended gospel number "That's the Way God Planned It." Ringo Starr even plays some drums for his mates and sings "It Don't Come Easy." Additional material on the bonus disc includes seventy-two minutes of documentaries, videos of the sound check, portions of the afternoon performance, and rehearsal footage of George and Dylan making constant eye contact while singing "If Not for You." "This will always be remembered as a time that we could be proud of being musicians," explained Clapton. "We weren't just thinking of ourselves for five minutes."

The ninety-nine-minute show earned $250,000 for UNICEF. The amount doesn't compare to Live Aid's tens of millions, but royalties from the movie and album are around $15 million. Now consumers can easily see why *The Concert for Bangladesh* became the model for decades' worth of relief efforts by rock stars.

The *Elevation 2001: Live from Boston* DVD is director Hamish Hamilton's two-disc set containing U2's performances from Boston's Fleet Center on June 5 and 6, 2001. Twenty different cameras were used to capture the events from all angles. Bono wore his black leather jacket, T-shirt, trousers, and sunglasses as he circled his heart-shaped walkway. After the huge, lavish spectacles of previous tours, U2 decided to tone things down a bit for Elevation's slightly more intimate shows in smaller venues. With a minimal stage design, U2 offers a healthy mix of new and old material, from "Beautiful Day" to "Sunday Bloody Sunday."

During the set's opener, "Elevation," the entire general admission floor hops up and down in unison with Bono. Under a strobe light during "Until the End of the World," the singer kicks the guitar in the Edge's hands, creating a memorable and dramatic affect. While the camera does capture unjustified crowd shots and jumps scenes frequently, it manages to focus on Bono and the other musicians for a fair length of time. Some highlights of the gig have been omitted, such as "Mysterious Ways" and "One." The latter comes as a surprise to U2 fans, considering the new poignancy "One" has taken on since the September 11, 2001, terrorist attacks.

The disc also contains a twenty-two-minute documentary on Elevation's production. The narrator, Tom Dunne, describes it as "organized chaos" in his Bono-like Irish accent. He describes the occasional conflicting goals of the film crew and concert production staff. One technician discusses being overwhelmed by the intellectual band, and explains why PopMart was "a lemon." Bono is shown speaking at a Harvard University graduation ceremony. "The only thing worse than a rock star is a rock star with a conscience. A celebrity with a cause; Oh my, oh my," he expresses to the audience. The second Elevation disc features a new high-tech perspective of the show. The DVD's "alternate camera" feature allows audience members to compare and contrast the view from the interactive "Bono Cam," the "Fan Cam," and the "Director Cam." There is also a five-minute "Road Movie" showing an empty arena being set up and then torn down after a U2 concert. Bonus songs include a thirty-second clip of "Zoo Station" in 1993. The entertainer is dressed as the Fly, smoking a cigarette in the Sydney stadium. Next, Bono is draped in a rope as he shadowboxes himself at Mexico City's PopMart show in 1997. "Elevation," the opening number of U2's first concert of the millennium, was shot in Miami's National Car Rental Center in March 2001. "Stuck in a Moment You Can't Get Out Of" was recorded live in Dublin's Clarence Hotel in 2000, and "Beautiful Day" features U2 on a Toronto rooftop the same year. The clip reminds viewers of the video for "Where the Streets Have No Name" filmed on top of a building, as well as the Beatles' "Get Back," the final song ever played live at an unannounced rooftop show in 1969. Finally, the DVD contains links to several home pages, such as Amnesty International and Greenpeace, for use on spectators' computers. It is obvious that the ONE Web site was yet to exist.

U2 Go Home: Live from Slane Castle in Ireland, released on DVD in 2003, is the band's best live performance available on the market. Playing for just over an hour and a half for an audience of almost a hundred and fifty thousand dancing on an open field with a terrific spirit is an astonishing sight. Kicking off with "Elevation" and "Beautiful Day," the set-list includes their first single, "Out Of Control," and some of their greatest hits, such as "New Year's Day" and "Pride." During the introduction of "Where the Streets Have No Name," Bono's operatic voice sounds unfamiliar and more like Pavarotti's than a rock-and-roll star. His interaction with the masses remains unmatched as he tells stories and jokes with the colossal crowd. Spectators can feel the undeniable energy that the crew omits from the stage. U2 appears so much more comfortable and natural than they do on the Boston DVD.

U2 Go Home includes a DVD-ROM with screensavers, desktop wallpapers, an Elevation tour calendar, Web links, and the possibility to view three different numbers from the show in a 360-degree perspective. "Mysterious Ways" appears as a bonus track, along with a remastered version of the *Unforgettable Fire* documentary from 1985. Viewers can watch the construction of a classic album.

Paul's 2002 DVD, *Back in the US*, mixes his concert footage from the previous year with documentary info. Paul explains in the film's opening credits that the tour's energy in the stands is comparable to the Beatles' hype, but it is no longer only sixteen-year-old girls in the audience. Under an enormous video monitor displaying the 1960s' British Invasion, the singer appears center stage in a blazer, T-shirt, and jeans. Besides Paul's red top and a matching lava lamp, everything on the massive platform is black, from the band's clothes to the instruments and the speakers.

With over three hours of live recordings, viewers get to see renditions of old and new favorites, including "Hello, Goodbye," "Jet," "Live and Let Die," "Eleanor Rigby," and an acoustic "Blackbird." Some fabulous favorites include "Something" and "Hey Jude," but they are only partially presented. While the sound quality is top-notch, the camerawork is extremely jumpy, with quick cuts of emotional men, women, and children in the crowd holding up Beatles paraphernalia.

The documentary includes the tour manager sharing aspects of his working life with the audience, while Paul's wardrobe lady displays his favorite outfits. Spectators are guided through Paul's dressing rooms, shower stall, after-show parties, and chartered jet. Individuals in the band relive their initial meetings with the billionaire, and fans from around the world discuss the concert experience. Additional special features include a set-list and the sound check performances of three different numbers, "Bring It to Jerome," "Midnight Special," and "San Francisco Bay." Finally, Sir Paul expresses in *Back in the US* that he has no urge to retire from the music industry, as he simply loves his job.

Although no U2 story compares to *The Beatles Anthology*, business-conscious reps released a collector's edition *How to Dismantle an*

Atomic Bomb CD set that includes a colorful hardback book with extracts from band members' notebooks, illustrations, photography, quotes, and statistics. There is also a documentary DVD featuring footage from the making of the album. "Sometimes You Can't Make It on Your Own," "Crumbs from Your Table," and "Vertigo" each feature Bono playing an acoustic guitar in the studio. In one of the two versions of "Vertigo," the Edge thumbs a banjo, giving the song a bluegrass feel. Throughout the second version, Bono dances in place and even mimics strangling himself with the microphone chord.

Each of the musicians discusses the three songs on the DVD. Bono expresses that U2's songwriting usually happens by accident. He claims the band don't really have a clue what they're doing, "and when we do, it doesn't seem to help." While Larry talks about the recording process in 2004, he certainly appears older than he did in 1988's baby-faced *Rattle and Hum*. Adam labels the process of picking one sound as "musical chairs." The Edge says that rock and roll is about the consistent energy of playing a guitar, as opposed to a keyboard. Bono confirms that the Edge is not a metallic guitarist and compares *How to Dismantle* to their first album.

The film closes with an outrageous but memorable quote from Bono. "Songs can change the world," he explains. "A song can change your mood, the temperature of the room you're in. Songs are incredible. . . . They become part of your life. They're more like smells, songs. They're a few bad smells out there of ours, but when we get it right, there's a scent. Freedom has a scent. And it's like the top of a newborn baby's head."

In 2005, an hour-long documentary, *U2: The Complete Story*, hit stores. The Irishmen's career is traced from their beginnings in Dublin to the top of the entertainment industry. The film appears to be made by amateurs using tasteless graphics and transitions. And there is minimal footage of the band. *The Complete Story* is simply long and uninteresting interviews of several random people associated with band. There ceases to be any concert footage or U2 music whatsoever. Every once in a while, a clip of a band member being interviewed in the 1980s surfaces on the screen. While the package comes with a discography and a trivia game called "Masterclass," the material offered is not worth the price of the blank DVD the documentary is recorded on.

As noted, in October 1993, Paul, George, and Ringo met in London to plan new recordings for an amazing release, *The Beatles Anthology*. They even asked Yoko for any of John's unreleased solo work that might be appropriate for overdubs, and she presented the boys with four of John's homemade demos; "Free as a Bird," "Real Love," "Grow Old with Me," and "Now and Then." By December of the same year, George Martin announced that *The Beatles Anthology* video release would be joined by a group-authorized book of their history, as well as eight audio discs compiled from four hundred hours of outtakes and never-before-distributed bootlegs on three two-audio-CD sets. Engineer Geoff Emerick mixed the material on a 1970 vintage analog eight-track disk with a restored acoustic echo chamber.

Fronting his eighth All-Starr Band since 1989, a cheerful Ringo performs sixteen numbers at Toronto's Casino Rama on the *Tour 2003* DVD. The lineup includes keyboard master Paul Carrack, guitarist Colin Hay, percussionist Sheila E., sax man Mark Rivera, and bass player John Waite in support of the 2003 release, *Ringorama*. Hits played at the show include Mike & The Mechanics' elegant "Living Years," Men At Work's radio-friendly "Down Under," and Sheila E.'s funk-pop "Glamorous Life."

Wearing a black satin button-down over a black T and blue jeans, Ringo appears tired when he performs "Honey Don't," "Boys," and "Yellow Submarine." He certainly does not have a million-dollar voice. The gang assists the Fab drummer in singing "With a Little Help from My Friends," and viewers get to watch a voluptuous Sheila E. grinding on the floor with a bass.

The disc also features unscripted up-close-and-personal backstage footage of Ringo introducing the event crew. The short documentary portrays the band with pre-show jitters, getting off of their private jet, and the former Beatle continuously joking with the cameraman. Dozens of still photos of the band jamming, as well as hanging out, are displayed in the "Tour Gallery." There is a Ringo Starr discography that begins with 1970's *Sentimental Journey*. Biographies on every band member give about seven paragraphs on each musician's career. Neither the performance nor the bonus features are particularly entertaining or interesting, and the *Tour 2003* DVD is a disappointment.

Jumping back decades to the 1981 spoof of prehistoric times, *Caveman*, Ringo plays the smallest and weakest one in his tribe. The character gets banished into the wilderness for having a crush on the chief of the tribe's busty mate. Starr eventually forms his own tribe of misfits, including Dennis Quaid and Shelley Long. The group discovers fire, cooking eggs, music making, and standing up straight. He and his followers escape deadly dinosaurs by using marijuana plants. *Caveman* is immature and its jokes are far from clever. Regardless, Ringo's comedy brings smiles to thousands.

Although no other movie in John's career compares to the quality of either *Imagine* or *The Beatles Anthology*, there are over one dozen films about the legend on the market. The year 1969's *Sweet Toronto* captures John, Yoko, and the Plastic Ono Band playing at the Peace Festival in Canada. The DVD remains Lennon's only filmed performance with the whole group. Another picture, *Sweet Toronto/Keep on Rockin'*, features classic footage of the same event, including the Plastic Ono Band playing with special guests Eric Clapton and Bo Diddley.

American Justice: The John Lennon Assassination was released in 1997. Host Bill Kurtis probes the sick mind of Mark David Chapman. The murder is examined through conversations with friends, attorneys, the arresting officer, and even Chapman himself from a prison cell.

The year 2000's *Gimme Some Truth: The Making of John Lennon's "Imagine" Album*, documents the man's most celebrated solo album. Incorporating footage from the original "Imagine," this film provides a taste of John's lifestyle, showing run-ins with Andy Warhol, Miles Davis, and Jack Nicholson. *In His Life* is a made-for-TV movie released the same year that explores John's rise to fame in the 1950s and '60s. Played by Philip McQullen, the young man gives up proper schooling in pursuit of becoming a professional musician. The poet's path is traced as he meets numerous artists before stumbling upon the other three Beatles.

Academy Award winner Kevin Spacey hosted *Come Together: A Night for John Lennon's Words and Music.* The all-star concert was broadcast live in 2002 from Radio City Music Hall as an extravagant tribute to New York City in the wake of the previous year's tragic events. Singing guests include Stone Temple Pilots, Alanis Morrissette, Cyndi Lauper, and Marc Anthony. *The Messenger* from 2002 documents John's career after the Beatles but provides no new information for viewers. However, *Inside John Lennon: Unauthorized*, released the following year, offers something different by including interviews with rare subjects, such as John's sister and members of his earlier group, the Quarrymen.

Lennon Legend, a DVD released in 2003, displays the Beatle's timeless influences on the world's mass media with twenty classic video clips, including "Imagine" and "Instant Karma." Two years later, the *John Lennon: Music Box Biographical Collection* retold his life story using rare archived footage. *Timeless Portrait*, yet another sketch honoring his career and legacy, was stocked in stores in 2006. Most recently, *The US vs. John Lennon* appeared on the big screen in 2006, focusing on Lennon's involvement in antiwar efforts and the US government's attempts to silence him. Yoko even collaborated on the making of this controversial film.

The 2006 DVD release *Paul McCartney: The Space Within Us* portrays the former Beatle's sold-out American jaunt throughout 2005. Utilizing more than two dozen cameras and 5.1 digital surround sound, the disc provides a front-row concert experience for the show. The performance was even beamed to the astronauts orbiting the Earth on the International Space Station who woke up to Paul's singles through a live feed from the tour during his Anaheim engagement.

The Space Within Us entails thirty timeless hits, such as the Beatles' "Magical Mystery Tour" and "Hey Jude." Wings' numbers included are "Maybe I'm Amazed" and well as "Too Many People." Solo material consists of an acoustic "Jenny Wren" and "English Tea." The movie also has special features, such "Paul's World":

short and to the point interviews with the band on Sir Paul's private jet. There is also an introduction by Cameron Crowe. The world-renowned director offers insight into the pop culture phenomenon that McCartney has represented for four decades. Crowds at the shows are of all ages, including those who were there for the Beatles' original appearance on *Sullivan* in 1964 and their children, mixed in with their grandkids.

Perhaps the most memorable of the moments on *The Space Within Us* occurred backstage in Miami, where the camera captures a short impromptu duet featuring Paul, James Taylor, and Tony Bennett. Local fans have expressed discontent about not witnessing the trio come together onstage. Regardless, there is nothing to complain about when it comes to the knight's new DVD, *The Space Within Us*.

U218 is 2006's compilation containing sixteen of the Irishmen's greatest hits, along with two additional cuts. It is the first collection to span the band's twenty-six-year career put on a single disc, from 1980's *Boy* to 2004's *How to Dismantle an Atomic Bomb*. The tracks skip around in chronological order of their recordings, as "Beautiful Day" is heard first. It includes two new releases. "The Saints are Coming" is U2's collaboration with Green Day yet to be on an album, and was actually recorded at the Beatles' Abbey Road Studios in London. Proceeds will benefit musicians affected by New Orleans' Hurricane Katrina. The second new release, "Window on the Sky," was also cut at Abbey Road. A bonus version of *U218* features a live DVD of ten songs performed at the 2005 Vertigo Tour's stop in Milan. Numbers experienced span from "I Will Follow" to the passionate "With or Without You" and "Elevation." It also includes a book with all of the lyrics, as well as priceless photos of the four dating back to the '70s. For any collector of quality singles, *U218* is a necessity.

By definition, a "bootleg" is an audio or video recording made, reproduced, or sold illegally without proper permission. The tracks are often copied and traded without money being exchanged, but some unscrupulous people are able to sell these rarities for profit after quality engineering and packaging to the raw tapes. The media is bought, sold, and traded at record collector shows, in smaller stores, on the street, and on countless Web sites. There are major bootleg markets online and in the streets of America, Europe, and Japan for groups such as KISS, the Rolling Stones, Zeppelin, U2, and of course, the Beatles.

The four British lads are one of the most bootlegged crews in music history. Ever since unlicensed records began hitting the market in the late 1960s, Beatles findings have appeared that were illegally recorded, stolen, or leaked from their production studio. Since the 1990s, bootleggers have made a point of attempting to make their releases look as legitimate as possible. Illegitimate CDs and videos began to overshadow the unauthorized vinyl.

For true Beatles fans on the hunt, hundreds of hours of previously unheard recordings can be found, as well as classic rock-and-roll covers. In the 1980s, engineer Geoff Emerick put together the numbers for an album of previously unreleased material that would be known as *Sessions*. The project never developed, but the tracks have appeared countless times in bootleg form. A majority of these finds, other studio takes, and talking in between songs appeared at the end of the decade on the *Ultra Rare Trax* series and *Unsurpassed Masters* CD collection. The "best" of the bootlegs were compiled in the 1990s and released in superior quality on the official, and legal, *The Beatles Anthology* CD series.

Beatles Bootlegs is a catalog of rare recordings, while BeatleLinks is an online database containing homemade audio files, a trading place, and more links to the Fab Four. On Bootleg Zone, visitors can choose from over thirty-five hundred pirated Beatle pieces online. Meanwhile, the site offers eighty-seven U2 boots. Achtung Bootlegs is a mini-site that blows its competition away, as it is made up of over two thousand unauthorized singles and reviews. Web surfers on the site can navigate in both French and English.

The U2 Bootleg Collector's Webring contains over twelve hundred songs on CDs, DVDs, and VCDs. The Silver and Gold site trades for Vertigo Tour bootlegs. U2 Boot Camp, U2 Holland, and Asmus U2 are just a few European sites that offer scarce recordings on CD, cassette, and PAL video. U2 Exit is a multimedia page made up of sound and video clips. Karlheinz's U2 Trading Page deals more than 250 shows on CD-ROM. U2 Rock Station features lyrics on top of its bartering, while For Love or Money is an online guide to unofficially released U2 material. Finally, U2 Bootleg Urban Legend Thread is the Internet's source for finding tickets to sold-out concerts.

"My feeling is that it is cool for people to share our music, as long as no one is making money from the process," Bono expressed on the U2 Bootlegs Web site. "We tell people who come to our concerts that they can tape the shows if they want. I think it is cool that people are so passionate about our music."[3]

The Edge is also quoted as saying, "The terror of online song-trading and bootlegging that has occurred in the wake of Napster is not something the members of U2 are losing any sleep over. In fact, as long as fans aren't being exploited and bootleggers aren't raking in huge money from the practice, it's a part of the music business they've come to accept."[4]

Any merchandise imaginable can be found in the Fest for Beatles Fans, the world's largest catalog of the band's products for purchase. The site is run out of New Jersey and accepts orders online "8 days a week" for its dwindling supplies. Consumers can choose between dozens of Beatles wristbands, shirts, jackets, hats, jewelry, blankets, foreign posters, stuffed animals, puzzles, shot glasses, cookie jars, lunch boxes, and Blue Meanie key chains.

Beatles-related posters come in all shapes and sizes, including John holding up a peace sign in front of the Statue of Liberty, a list detailing the band's history, US albums illustrated with multicolor lithography, giant door hangings, and hand-numbered prints in black and white of Astrid Kirchherr's photography including twelve previously unpublished photos of George in 1961. Three different gold-plated records with Lennon photos are also up for grabs.

Fab shirts are available in every conceivable size and color, from children's apparel with the Beatles cartoons and Sgt. Pepper glitter to zipper "Hoodie" jackets, tie-dyes containing catchy slogans from the British Invasion. Buyers can also grab Ts with V-necks, psychedelic photos, and souvenirs of the 1964 American tour in Candlestick Park.

Similarly, *Propaganda*, the one and only official magazine devoted to U2, was printed monthly from 1986 until 2000. But more than just merchandise, the periodical supplied band news, interviews, and photography. There is still a home page online, www.u2propaganda.com, featuring words of wisdom from the band, their staff, and their followers. These days, the Propaganda link connects readers to U2.com. Internet surfers will also find U2 write-ups regularly on both the Amnesty International and Greenpeace Web pages.

The U2.com shop carries a wide range of Vertigo 2005 merchandise for sale. From key chains for under ten dollars to subway-size concert posters and vintage Ts from Europe, the Irish band's Web site offers it all. One top item for sale is the benefit shirt worn by Edge during U2's Grammy performance. It features a Music Rising design and logo, a charity benefiting musicians after hurricanes Katrina and Rita devastated the Gulf Coast in 2005.

In 2004, U2 partnered up with Apple Computer's innovative iPod, a minute device that holds up to five thousand songs. The U2 player features a custom engraving of the band members' signatures. Redefining music with technology in the new digital age, U2 can now have online relationships with their audience. In the summer of 2006, *Rolling Stone* claimed that the Beatles catalog will make it online "in the not-too-distant future," and in early 2007, CNET News.com claimed it will be available soon. "The Beatles music will one day be downloading," said a computer-lingo-challenged Ringo.[5]

There are countless books on the Beatles, and most of them focus on the accomplishments of the group as a whole. Other volumes examine the exploits of John and Paul, and to a lesser extent, George, followed by Ringo. Cynthia Lennon, the Beatle's first wife, wrote a biography, *John*, describing him in a negative tone. John tried to suppress the Englishwoman's first book on her legendary ex-husband, *A Twist of Lennon*, in 1978 on grounds of libel. In her second piece of nonfiction, Cynthia inspects the same relationship with John from his college years as an art student, up to their divorce in 1969, and the post-Beatle years. Shedding an unfavorable light on the man, *John* chronicles the transformation of an innocent lad from Liverpool in the 1950s to an iconoclastic figure after his murder in 1980.

Cynthia offers never-before-heard tales of her originally falling for John and trapping him into marriage. She recounts later painful episodes in their lives, including his role as a husband and as a father, as well as in-depth information about John's Aunt Mimi and sisters, Julia and Jacqui. The writer vividly depicts John's most mundane everyday faults, such as being an irresponsible shopper. Cynthia also complains that he had "no interest in legal matters and always left them to others."[6] Cynthia blames LSD for the failure of their marriage, as an addicted John became lost from reality by 1967. She also points her finger at Yoko Ono for John's distance from, and neglect of, his family after he moved to New York City in the early '70s. Most interesting is Cynthia's account of John first meeting the Japanese artist at an exhibition in central London.

John combines a handful of familiar photos of the young guitarist, with some new, never before published, ones of the Beatles' teenage years. Cynthia also submitted a couple of interesting drawings of her wedding to Lennon in 1962 and their honeymoon in Paris, as there was no camera present at either of the events.

The book concludes with a discussion of John's murder and his sons' inheritance. Cynthia questions whether John would have been knighted by the queen, like Paul, Mick Jagger, and Elton John were, if he were alive today. In her memorable closing words, Cynthia states, "If I'd known as a teenager what falling for John Lennon would lead to, I would have turned round right then and walked away."[7]

Cynthia and John's son, Julian, penned the manuscript's short but poignant introduction. Julian attempts to educate Beatles fans of the significant role in John's life that his mother played from his school days to the birth of the Beatles. He discusses the difficulties of growing up as the son of a Beatle and relives his feelings of rejection from John. Julian explains that his father wasn't much of a hero in his eyes. Rather, John was a disappointing parent, as Julian relives "the truth, the real truth, about Dad's life."[8]

Larry Kane, a journalist who traveled with the Beatles on their 1964 invasion of the States, recounted the experience in *Ticket to Ride*. His 2005 *Lennon Revealed* assesses John, his private life, career, and murder from a personal standpoint. Kane utilized personal and honest recollections, along with interviews with many of the superstar's friends and associates to tell the story of how John "blazed a decisive course in cultural history."[9]

Pivotal moments in John's personal and professional lives are shared, revealing several facets of the complex celebrity. In the chapter "All You Need Is Love," Lennon's childhood and early romances are explored. Kane also discusses the band's highly protected public image in the cultural spotlight, describing the boys as "clean-cut and fabulously well-behaved."[10] John shares his blatant feelings about politics, the peace movement, and the war in Vietnam with the journalist as well. The final chapter of *Lennon Revealed* is a collection of letters to the icon written by his fans. Titled "The Lennon Generations Speak," the section feels out of place; it does not connect to the rest of the book.

Geoffrey Giuliano is the author of thirty-six books, including *The Beatles: A Celebration*, as well as a biography on George. He has also written numerous articles for *Rolling Stone*, *Music Scene*, and *Playgirl*, while serving as a contributing editor of *Beatlefan* magazine. In 1986, Paul was interviewed, along with George, Yoko, Julian Lennon, and Pete Best, for Giuliano's next project, the 1991 *Blackbird: The Life and Times of Paul McCartney*. The book spans four decades as it touches upon Paul's relationships with the other Beatles, his thousands of fans, and the press on both sides of the Atlantic. He explores Paul's years as a teenager, as a Beatle, and their rise to global success.

Blackbird offers no new information to readers. Everything reported is old news, such as the band's first appearance on *Sullivan* and the murderous tale to follow "Helter Skelter." Giuliano explains the turmoil surrounding their final studio album, the memorable *Abbey Road* sessions, originally entitled *Everest*, in 1969.

McCartney also discusses his up-and-down relationship with John, mentioning their "fortuitous first" encounter in 1957, as well as facing his lifelong friend and working partner's murder.[11] There are in-depth descriptions of two of the most important women in the Beatles' careers. The initial meeting with the sweet Linda McCartney is discussed, along with her marriage to Paul. Linda is then compared to "the snaky, condescending Yoko."[12]

Giuliano describes John's smile "from ear to ear" when he, George, and Ringo tossed "two perfectly new bricks" at Paul's estate. The incident took place immediately after McCartney petitioned the London High Court to order the Beatles' partnership dissolved.

Paul's career without the Beatles in the 1970s entailed a joint venture with Linda in Wings. The busy couple also gave birth to four children. Most interesting is the story behind the Wings tour being cancelled when the famous couple spent nine days in a Japanese prison. Flying into the country, customs discovered a "fist-sized plastic bag obviously containing several ounces of pot" in the McCartneys' luggage.[13] Details are also examined on Paul's solo work in the 1980s, enhanced by his working relationships with stars such as Michael Jackson and Elvis Costello.

Along with the book's fantastic photos of Paul's bands and his family, the book's *greatest* contribution to Fab fans is an interview with Paul conducted at a preshow press conference during McCartney's 1989–1990 world tour. He discusses the immeasurable feeling of performing Beatles songs live for the first time ever in the 1980s, as popular tunes such as "Sgt. Pepper's Lonely Hearts Club Band" and "Hey Jude" were written and recorded after the band stopped touring. Paul also claimed that a Beatles reunion "is out of the question because John is not with us."[14] A 1997 volume includes an updated discography, excerpts from interviews, the musician's animal rights efforts, the band members reuniting for work on the *Anthology* albums, and Linda's losing battle against breast cancer.

George Harrison is the only Beatle to write an autobiography. Taken from intense transcripts with the Beatles press officer, Derek

Taylor, the 1980 *I Me Mine* was initially released in a high-priced limited edition. The updated version includes an introduction by George's widow, Olivia, which is quite endearing. She explains the title, the memories that the book induces in her, and some of George's most inspirational findings. He was stirred by both Hinduism as well as ideal vacation spots such as Maui. The book tells very little about the Beatles. Rather, *I Me Mine* focuses on Harrison's pastimes, such as gardening and Formula One auto racing.

The four-hundred-page memoir is written in three parts. The first is George's brief, but fresh and humorous, compilation of growing up in Liverpool, discovering rock and roll, and meeting the other Beatles. George recounts manager Brian Epstein telling the cocky band, "You're going to be bigger than Elvis" in 1964.[15] The second section of *I Me Mine* includes the lyrics to over eighty of Harrison's songs, many of which were scribbled on scratch paper with corrections intact, offering short histories and witty explanations to fans. Finally, there is a collection of illustrations and roughly fifty rare black-and-white photographs with quirky captions.

Random information in the book includes his childhood fear of joining the military. The early success of the band in 1964 is brought to light, as George compares it to the "Cuckoo's Nest."[16] He claims that he would never want to live through the chaos again. Other fun facts: George loved of India, and also Monty Python's version of the Beatles, the Rutles. George's autobiography is a must-have for a Beatles follower, as the funny lines, artifacts, and photos are truly unique.

Ringo Starr is usually passed over when biographies are written on individual Beatles, so a book recounting the oldest Beatle's life should be a worthy addition to any fan's bookshelf. However, Alan Clayson's *Ringo Starr: Straight Man or Joker* from 1992 is a bitter disappointment, lacking insight and emotion.

In *Straight Man or Joker*, Clayson follows the drummer through his entire career as a musician in Liverpool, as an actor, and ending with his first All-Starr Band tour. Topics explored include romantic interests, unsteady health issues, and alcoholism. Apparently, the man was forced to give up drinking before he "died in hell like

Elvis."[17] Ringo was chosen to replace percussionist Pete Best in 1962 and was forced to mature in the midst of Beatlemania. The bedlam of the band's tours, drug use, side projects, and disagreements are each mentioned randomly throughout the book.

The drummer's life in the 1970s, '80s, and '90s is less chronicled than his days as a mop top. The 1973 solo album *Ringo* is explored, along with his later releases. Clayson states that the solo Ringo project is the closest that the Fab Four ever came to a full reunion, as John, Paul, and George each contributed work separately on various tracks. Fans learn about the assortment of music that Ringo appreciates, ranging from Jerry Lee Lewis to Led Zeppelin. There is also the interesting tale of George's outburst at dinner, claiming his love for Ringo's wife, Maureen Cox. Following 1983's *Old Wave* solo record, Ringo took an absence from the spotlight for several years.

Ringo reappeared in 1989 with the first lineup of the All-Starr Band. Featuring Joe Walsh, Billy Preston, and other big-name celebrities of the industry, the band hit the road, selling out a series of venues in the United States. Plugs on *Good Morning America* and *The David Letterman Show* are touched on, along with the aging pop singer's guest voice appearances in Hollywood, as well as on an episode of *The Simpsons* in the '90s. Along with odd factual tidbits, the biography's greatest addition for Beatles fans is a priceless photo of Ringo as Sir Elton John tries to plant a kiss on his face. Ringo has spent recent decades performing in countless partnerships with everyone from Bob Dylan and Keith Richards to Eric Clapton and Van Morrison. But Clayson immediately loses credibility as a writer when he refers to Ireland's Van Morrison as "British."[18]

Clayson did not interview Ringo, his family members, ex-girlfriends, or musicians who worked closely with the world's most famous drummer. Pete Best apparently gave Clayson an interview, as he is much of the book's focus. The author utilized existing biographies, along with articles from magazines and newspapers. *Straight Man or Joker* drags out and is anything but educational or exciting for Beatles fans.

On the twenty-fifth anniversary of John's death, Yoko solicited material from seventy-three of Lennon's friends, contemporaries, and admirers for an artistic collection of their reminiscences. Some celebrities memorialize the man in poetry or song, and others depict John in art. While the cover design was crafted by John himself in 1979, Yoko penned the touching introduction. Lennon's widow claims that she still isn't ready to write an autobiography about her life with John, twenty-five years after his death.[19]

A sketch of John was drawn by a twelve-year-old Bono. The caption under the work reads, "Oh my Lord, Love for the first time in my life . . . I could see." Lennon's music obviously helped the Irish child put his strong feelings from the heart into words, poetry, and song.[20] Giving praise, Sir Mick Jagger discusses his first encounter and ongoing friendship with John through 1960s and '70s. Carlos Santana explains what Lennon and the song "Imagine" mean to the entire world, and the B-52s' singer Kate Pierson attests to seeing him as "practically a mythological figure."[21] Journalist Norman Mailer wrote one heartfelt line, and both producer David Geffen and Pete Townshend wrote pages about John's influence on their careers. Townshend states that "pop poetry is of doubtful value" if singers such as Bono and Bob Geldof don't actually benefit mankind.[22] Cynthia O'Neal, Lennon's neighbor at the Dakota, recounts the day he was shot in the apartment building's entryway. Memorable quotes on John's death are also contributed by Sir Elton John and Chuck Berry. Touching pieces are included from photographer Annie Leibovitz's historic work from her last session with John and Yoko. The enlightening pictures entail the icon and his wife wearing the same sunglasses, hairstyles, and nothing whatsoever. Beatles fans may be disappointed that contributions from Paul, Ringo, and Cynthia are absent from *Memories of John Lennon*.

Lacking the same visual presentation, *Bono: In His Own Words* is full of intensely personal quotes from the singer during U2's first decade in the spotlight. Journalist Dave Thompson compares U2 to other Irish acts Van Morrison, Thin Lizzy, and the Boomtown Rats, while supplying insight to Bono's personality.

The pop star offers his feelings on U2, other bands, and the fame game. One hundred pages explain the singer's history and his newly achieved celebrity status with quotes backed by black-and-white photographs.

In 1980, Bono expressed why his band wouldn't relocate to London. "My whole entry into London, going down into the tube, all the ads were underpants, neon signs, prostitution, masturbation, people hurrying to get places, traffic going so fast. . . . I said no, I didn't feel part of it already, that's not for us."[23]

"What I want from music are people who lay themselves on the line. People like John Lennon or Iggy Pop did that. Whatever you feel about their music, you do learn about them from it," Bono said in 1983.[24]

Music journalist Michka Assayas first reported on U2 for the Paris-based magazine *Le Monde de la musique*. In the last two and a half decades, the writer, who has continuously worked with the band members, conducted a series of intimate interviews with their front man. Released in 2005, *Bono in Conversation with Michka Assayas* offers the Irishman's "long answers to short questions . . . always in the pursuit of truth" from a first-person perspective.[25] Topics inside the collection shift in a nonlinear fashion from the singer's relationships with his wife and his father, as well as the affiliation between those two, to Bono opening up about religion in his house growing up and his personal stories as a confused teenager. He touches on growing old and discusses planning his own funeral. Bono even shares conversations that occur between him and God.

Assayas gives little background about U2, as Bono reflects on his evolving entertainment career and as an activist. The celebrity declares that the groundbreaking Zoo TV tour has been labeled "the *Sgt. Pepper* of live shows."[26] He also talks in detail about historical figures in his life, his personal views on Martin Luther King Jr. and Bobby Kennedy. The ongoing fight against AIDS in Africa is touched upon, as well as Bono's memorable meeting with a cigar-puffing Bill Clinton inside the Oval Office.

Bono in Conversation with Michka Assayas does not mention U2's outrageous stories from the studio or the road. The intimate journey into Bono's head ceases to get emotional, even when the singer reflects upon his recently deceased father. Rather, the entertaining book gives insight to the quick-witted and humble superstar. For example, Bono explains that he has always found himself in other people, such as his father and John Lennon.

In the early 1980s, Paul began the artistic process of exploring with a paintbrush. A remarkable spirit and visual cleverness were suddenly discovered on canvas. In 2000, an intriguing portfolio of work entitled *Paul McCartney Paintings* was published. The colorful book is a catalog of 117 vivid, exuberant, and complex illustrations from the celebrity's 1999 exhibition in Germany. Abstract expressionism, blobs, and splatters of paint inspire the craft. The Beatle's creative touches vary from open landscapes with dynamic colors to cute, cartoonlike figures with symbolic value. The subjects animated range from the queen of England and Paul's late wife, Linda, to Celtic motifs and a representation of "a great penis," as well as "someone bending down, facing away from you."[27]

Accompanying humorous essays, contemporary critiques, and candid interviews with the insightful Paul are matched with Linda's photos of the artist and his influential mentor, Willem de Kooning. Along with several of the pieces' personal meanings, Paul discusses a few insecurities and defining moments in his diverse career.

Brian Clarke reports that Paul has used his creativity on canvas to distinguish "himself as historically as he has in the cultural landscape of the century as a songwriter and performer."[28] Later in the collection, Paul confirms that the greatest advice he ever received from other craftsmen was "Paint more."[29]

Doodling with a lighter tone, John's *Real Love: The Drawings for Sean* hit bookstores in 1999. Unlike his half-brother Julian Lennon, Sean spent years growing up with his indulgent father in their Dakota apartment in New York City. In fact, the former art student put his musical career on hold to focus on fatherhood. John and his son spent time playing together by etching animals and creating captions from Sean's immediate reactions. Years later,

Yoko put together the touching work and wrote an introduction to the forty-eight-page collection.

While the medium is never identified as pen, ink, chalk, or crayon, *Real Love: The Drawings for Sean* entails John's simple and playful line sketches. There are dozens of different creatures playing together, along with humorous descriptions that give the book personality. Viewers can feast their eyes on a sleeping cartoon cat, a frog reflecting over a puddle, and a sleepy elephant counting sheep, along with other *Sesame Street*–like cartoons. In the book's foreword, Yoko explains, "That's how Sean learned the fun of drawing, the fun of doing things together with his dad, and the fun of life."[30]

Much like John's barnyard animals, Bono put together the images by hand for 2003's publication of Sergei Prokofiev's *Peter and the Wolf*. Bono and his two daughters, Jordan and Eve, have supplied the designs for the delightful new version of the famous story first printed in 1936. The box set includes a clothbound book with sixty-four pages of original representations. There is also an enhanced CD of the story being performed by the funny Gavin Friday and the Friday-Seezer Ensemble. Royalties from the new millennium's *Peter and the Wolf* are benefiting the Irish Hospice Foundation. In 2004, several more of the singer's childlike paintings and sketches were printed on the inside pages of the album insert for *How to Dismantle an Atomic Bomb*.

George did not paint or draw, but Ringo is the third sketch artist of the Beatles. While on tour in the late '90s, the drummer began experimenting with a painting program and creating computer art. Beginning with simple designs, Ringo purchased an electronic drawing pad and taught himself to paint electronically through trial and error. The titles are simple, such as "Hat Man." Just about every one of the pieces depicts a face, close-up, wearing a cap. Like Ringo himself, the work is playful and quirky. He takes no monies from the sale of his art. In the summer of 2005, the first public exhibition of Ringo's computer art went on display at Pop International Galleries in New York City's SoHo. All of the profits benefit the Lotus Foundation Charity, offering financial aid to family and child welfare, women's issues, animal protection, addiction recovery, and education.

Web sites are essential these days for a band to keep on top of the market. The Beatles.com Web site allows followers to stay up to date by receiving news and finding short information on the group's history, records, and movies. As expected, Beatles.com contains links to several other similar home pages, as well as ONE.org. The introduction page quotes *Fifty Years Adrift*, Derek Taylor's book recalling a concert experience. Though it is made up of fantastic animation, educated fans will not gain any new knowledge about the Beatles on the site.

On the Beatles.com home page, visitors can connect to a page on Cirque du Soleil's *LOVE* at no cost. On June 30, 2006, over four thousand guests attended the opening night in Las Vegas. The Mirage began featuring an intimate reproduction of the Fab Four's history onstage. Sixty international artists relive music history inside *LOVE*'s state-of-the-art venue with 360-degree seating, panoramic video projections, and surround sound. Following the emotional hour and a half show, a standing ovation continued as Paul, Ringo, Yoko, Olivia Harrison, and Sir George Martin stepped up onstage. Paul successfully requested "just one special round of applause" for John and George.

LOVE brings the vivid magic of Cirque du Soleil together with the timeless spirit and intimate messages of the Beatles. Born from a mutual friendship and admiration between the late George Harrison and Cirque founder Guy Laliberté, the entertainment experience entails a spectacular feast for both the eyes and ears. The custom-built theatre at the Mirage in Las Vegas was the former home to Siegfried and Roy. There are sixty international artists onstage, sometimes dressed in *Sgt. Pepper's* outfits, doing nonstop acrobatics on trampolines, slides, disappearing into hidden compartments, and flying high through the air. Two television monitors at the top of the arena display never-before-seen videos and rare photos of the Fab Four.

Using the master tapes at Abbey Road Studios, both familiar and lesser-known original tunes create *LOVE*'s amazing soundtrack.

Over two dozen phenomenal numbers are used, ranging from "Hey Jude," "A Day in the Life," and "Tomorrow Never Knows" to the less popular "Cry Baby Cry" and "Glass Onion." There is a reading of the poetic lyrics to "Blackbird" with no music in the background. George's sweet ballad "Something" is the surprising highlight of the performance.

There's something in the way the dancers move around the stage that encourages visitors to the Vegas Strip to treat themselves to the richness of *LOVE*. Free your mind to the unforgettable set, urban freestyle dance, aerial gymnastics, and immortal music. Tickets range from sixty-nine to a hundred and fifty bucks a pop.

Visitors of www.beatlesmuseum.nl can compare the band's European singles, bootleg albums, books, and magazines with those released to the rest of the world. Based out of a shop a half an hour north of Amsterdam in Alkmaar, the collected works also feature the Beatles' original contracts, paintings, autographs, and clothing. Seven-inch Records at www.7inchrecords.com is the commercial site of the Beatles Museum for consumers seeking rare vinyl collections. Meanwhile, memorabilia can be purchased at the Beatles Fan Shop next door to the museum, and guests may treat themselves to a cup in Eleanor Rigby's Tea Room.

Dozens of similar Web sites exist, including the Belgian Beatles Society, as well as others that focus on the band's findings for sale and even listing of the top hundred Fab home pages. Rather than merely in Britain, these sites do business all over the world, from the United States and Australia to China, the Netherlands, and Ireland.

U2.com contains the most information and deluxe features of all the bands' Web sites. Of course, only paid subscribers gain access to all the site has to offer, such as discounts on U2 merchandise and a personal Web address at U2.com. Features include news, singles, audio, video archives, photo galleries, lyrics, a timeline, personal interviews, a mailing list, tour listings, and a store, as well as pages of fan's personal concert reviews. There are special video exclusives, including a half-hour segment of Bruce Springsteen inducting U2 into the Rock and Roll Hall of Fame and specially commissioned behind-the-scenes tour footage.

Once a person becomes a paid member ($40 per year in America, and $32 for resubscribers), a bonus gift will be mailed to the subscriber's home. In the spring of 2006, the gift was U2.Communication, an audio disc of eight U2 tracks performed live on the Vertigo tour. The songs are matched with an interactive CD-ROM allowing users to create their own playlists. Distinctive wallpapers, screensavers, and a live video of the concert in Milan are on the disc as well.

The Bono Online Web site at www.bonoonline.com contains random photos, videos, news articles, and just about anything else imaginable to do with the Irishman. Fans from the WebPages's forum flew to Dublin in the summer of 2006 to deliver a scrapbook to Bono's house. The gift contained hundreds of letters, followers' photos with the band, poetry, and artwork of U2, along with small gifts as tokens of appreciation for all of their hard work.

Additional Web sites dedicated to the band are U2Star with a wonderful forum for fans, and U2Tours, which focuses on life on the road. U2Wanderer supplies all the band's discography and lyrics, while @U2 features amazing cartoons. Still, fans can find just about anything they'll ever be looking for on U2.com.

Hundreds of sites around the world have links to ONE.org, an effort by Americans to rally other citizens of every walk of life to fight global AIDS and extreme poverty. The organization of over two million and its Web site focuses on Africa's debt cancellation by aiming to help Americans raise their voice. By using celebrity spokesmen and women, ONE aims to allocate an additional 1 percent of the US budget, approximately $25 billion, toward health, education, clean water, and food in the world's poorest countries. In 2006, less than 1 percent of the federal budget was allocated for fighting AIDS and food deficiencies around the world. The overall goal of ONE is for America to demonstrate its commitment to the Millennium Goals, an internationally agreed-upon effort to cut global hunger in half by 2015.

There are twenty-six chapters in J. D. Salinger's *The Catcher in the Rye*, the inspirational book Mark David Chapman was carrying immediately after shooting John Lennon. Peace Arch Entertainment is a Canadian-based company that released *Chapter 27*, a dramatic depiction of the killer's days leading up to the infamous shooting on December 8, 1980. The independent release was intended to be an exploration of the shooter's psyche, without emphasizing John's actual death in front of the Dakota apartment complex where Yoko still lives.

Written and directed by Jarrett Schaeffer, his first film was released in March of 2007 after much controversy. Jared Leto, also seen as a heroin addict in *Requiem for a Dream*, gained sixty-seven pounds for the role of the murderer in New York City. Chapman is presently serving a prison sentence of twenty years to life. Lindsay Lohan stars as Jude, a friend of the convict and a devoted Beatles follower. The actress met with Yoko several times to discuss the part, as Yoko controls both the rights to the man's music and movie rights to the registered trademark known as "John Lennon." Both Leto and Lohan received death threats for their parts in *Chapter 27*.

Although some commentators viewed *Chapter 27* as an opportunity to educate the world further on the beloved rock star, thousands have boycotted the picture. Protestors claim that the exposure is exactly what the villain was seeking by his brutal actions and desecrates the memory of John. Web sites were created for fans to share their feelings on *Chapter 27*. Ideas expressed include giving the rights of the screenplay to a master of depicting real-life scenarios, such as Martin Scorsese or Oliver Stone. The acting, the editing, and the soundtrack would be phenomenal. But the independent-minded directors of superstar stature would never collaborate with someone like Yoko, as she would demand final control of the picture. When the woman does grant permission for a production replicating her deceased husband's life, it is to less-known artists at whom she can bark orders. Such was the case in 2005 with Don Scardino, writer and director of the short-lived Broadway musical *Lennon*.

Other Hollywood depictions about the fallen hero include *The Hours and Times* from 1991. The role of the musician, with his alleged affair with Brian Epstein, is played by Ian Hart. The same actor was cast a second time as Lennon in 1994's *Backbeat*, a flick portraying the Beatles in Hamburg in the early 1960s. A fictional reunion between John and Paul a few years after the band split is represented in 2000's *The Two of Us*. Regardless of the number of features recounting Lennon's life and death, none has received the controversial publicity of *Chapter 27*.

12

The Icons
Come Together

LIVE 8 WITH A LITTLE HELP
FROM SOME FRIENDS

LIVE AID WAS HELD in London's Wembley Stadium in mid-July 1985 and at Philadelphia's JFK Stadium to raise money for the seven million victims of hunger in Ethiopia. One in every three people was dying in the modern-day famine. Endorsed by MTV, the cultural event featured many of the biggest stars of the time, bringing in over $100 million. Like Band Aid, Live Aid was the brainchild of Midge Ure, along with the multitalented actor from *The Wall*, *NME* journalist, and lead singer of the Boomtown Rats, Bob Geldof. The sixteen-hour marathon became a truly historic event, as the gig was broadcast live to over a billion people worldwide.

Headliners taking part in the original Live Aid included Paul McCartney, U2, Bob Dylan, Elton John, Mick Jagger, David Bowie, Phil Collins, and Queen. Each act had been allocated a slot of no more than twenty minutes, leaving each with an opportunity to perform only their best-known songs. The gargantuan undertaking involved a revolving stage split into three segments. While one section was for the band playing, the second was for the next crew to set up their equipment, while the third was for the act who just finished playing to dismantle their gear.

At the original show, Paul's microphone didn't come on until halfway through "Let It Be," though he didn't know it at the time. Sir Paul still wanted his performance to be included on the new DVD but needed to rerecord his singing. In order to cover up the visuals of the technical problem, he is shown at his piano from the back of the stage only for the first half of the song. Otherwise, his lips, as well as the mouths of the entire Wembley Stadium audience, would have been out of synch with the new DVD's audio track. Viewers can tell exactly when the concert's technicians fixed the problem, as they can see Paul's face, as well as catch the crowd explode with approval when they finally hear his original vocals. By the end of the Beatles' classic, David Bowie, the Who's Pete Townshend, and Bob Geldof strolled onstage to join Paul. Coincidently, Paul also sang "Let It Be" at the benefit Concert for the People of Kampuchea in 1979. Mr. McCartney organized the event to raise money for the victims of Pol Pot's reign of terror in Cambodia.

Much of the world, as noted, got their first look at U2 during Live Aid. Actor Jack Nicholson introduced the Irishmen via satellite from America: "A group whose heart in is Dublin, Ireland; whose spirit is with the world; a group that's never had any problem telling the world how they feel, U2."

Denying the crowd of thousands a prologue, U2 played an astonishing version of "Sunday Bloody Sunday." Dressed in a Confederate soldier's jacket, a white button-down with a bolo western cowboy shoestring tie, leather slacks, and enormous black boots, the singer jumped all around the stage. The cameramen did their best to keep up with his constant motion onstage. "You know the words," Bono explained under enormous 1980s hair with highlights. He requested the spectators to "Sing 'No more, no more.'"

In a much thicker Irish accent than audiences in the twenty-first century are used to, Bono explained, "We're an Irish band. We've come from Dublin City, Ireland. Like all cities, it has its good and it has its bad." The singer serenaded the crowd with Lou Reed's "Satellite of Love" during the introduction of "Bad."

Halfway through the number, Bono dropped the mic and began sprinting around the stage. He jumped into the sectioned-off security pit between the audience and the stage, pulling out a lucky young lady from the front row to dance with. "Bad" consisted of a medley including the Rolling Stones' "Ruby Tuesday" and "Sympathy for the Devil," as well as Reed's "Walk on the Wild Side." Viewers can easily see how hard Bono and his band were trying to connect with the audience in the mid-'80s, a task they carried out with ease twenty years later. The twenty-five-year-old singer's stage presence and his youthful voice were maturing in front of a global audience of millions.

By the time Paul and Pete Townshend carried an exhausted Geldof on their shoulders at the end of the show, over $70 million had been raised worldwide, topped by $140 million in royalties. The Live Aid concert event was witnessed on television by millions of people. DVD sales of the Live Aid concert grossed more than two million pounds in England.

"Being the Batman and Robin of rock and roll has its disadvantages," the Edge explained to *Rolling Stone*'s James Henke in 1988. "What we are, first and foremost, is a rock-and-roll band. If we forget that, people are going to stop listening. So at the moment my feeling is that I don't really want to do any charity shows for the moment. I think it would devalue anything else we've done."[1]

Unlike Live Aid, the historic Live 8 wasn't intended to raise money but rather awareness, as well as to apply political pressure for the issue of global poverty, to promote fair trade, and to get the richest nations to cancel debts. Numerous concerts were held simultaneously on July 2 and one on July 6, 2005. The monstrous event took place in London, Paris, Rome, Berlin, Toronto, and Philadelphia. The concerts were planned to precede the G8 Conference and Summit held at Gleneagles in Scotland scheduled later that week. Live 8 was held on the twentieth anniversary of Live Aid.

More than a thousand musicians participated in Live 8, many of whom had been out of the public eye for years. Performances were shown on a 182 television networks and heard on two thousand radio stations. Millions of viewers watched the event labeled "the greatest show on Earth." The nine Live 8 concerts were shown on big screens in seven cities across the United Kingdom, and broadcast live on BBC TV and radio.

At the London show, Elton John said he was extremely honored to be taking part in Live 8, which also featured some of the most respected names in the industry. Classic rockers the Who, shared a bill with Sting, George Michael, Madonna, Annie Lennox, Mariah Carey, Velvet Revolver, Coldplay, and R.E.M. Along with reggae superstars UB40, Snoop Dogg rapped about life on the streets. The show in London featured a historic reunion of Pink Floyd, including bassist and lyricist Roger Waters.

Rumor has it that Paul McCartney refused to play London's Live 8 unless he got to both open and close the show. His request was granted, and Paul played a set consisting solely of Beatles songs. Kicking off the event in London's Hyde Park, Sir Paul took the stage with Bono to sing the classic "Sgt. Pepper's Lonely Hearts Club Band." Above the stage, a giant sign spelled out "One Voice to Make Poverty History." On Live 8's backdrop, photos and videos of celebrities were projected, including Lennon, Dylan, and Abraham Lincoln. Onstage, Paul wore a simple black T-shirt with blue jeans and Bono was draped in a black denim jacket, black T, black jeans, and his trademark sunglasses. McCartney sang the opening verse of the song, then Bono joined in with the chorus and also chanted the second verse. The two icons were backed by a horn section made up of four Beatles look-alikes dressed in colorful Sgt. Pepper's uniforms. "*Imagine*, what a trip! Paul McCartney, what a gift to the world," Bono expressed to thousands.

Paul departed and then U2 took charge with "Beautiful Day." Midway through the song, dozens of white doves were released into the sky from the front of the stage. Bono altered the cities mentioned in "Beautiful Day's" lyrics to match the cities hosting Live 8, such as Philadelphia and Berlin. The number wound down with U2 singing slightly rearranged lyrics to a Beatles classic. "Blackbird singing in the dead of night / Take these sunken eyes and learn to see. / All your life / You were only waiting for this moment to arise. / Blackbird Fly," Bono sang. However, he should have expressed, "*You were only waiting for this moment to be free.*" Paul didn't seem to mind.

The crowd roared and Bono confronted his audience. "Alright now, this is a rock and roll show. A hip-hop show." He borrowed a phrase from one of 1985's numbers, "Bad," questioning, "How long? How long?" As Bono began counting out of order in the intro to *Atomic Bomb*'s "Vertigo," he added a profanity to the lyrics in front of thousands: "Just give us what we fuckin' want, and no one gets hurt." The sign above the stage changed its message to "We Don't Want Your Money. We Want You." U2's historical performance at Live 8 came to a close with Bono singing an acoustic version of "One."

Following the Who and Pink Floyd's performances hours later, Paul returned. "Hey, Hyde Park, you are beautiful," he expressed. "You've come for the right reasons." Now wearing a black blazer over his white shirt and jeans, Paul ripped into "Helter Skelter." Spectators were surprised that Bono didn't appear again to help steal back the song. Above trippy lights and cartoons, the sign changed again: "Live 8—The Long Walk to Justice," followed by "Live 8. G8. Be Great."

Paul asked his audience if they've had a great day. Tens of thousands were still cheering when George Michael joined the "cute one" onstage for the Otis Redding–influenced Beatles classic, "Drive My Car." Paul then asked, "Do you want to rock some more? I want to rock some more. We rock and roll and stomp and stroll all the way to Edinburgh."

Paul took a seat behind a grand piano and fingered 1970's pop ballad "The Long and Winding Road." A little before midnight, he led straight into Live 8's memorable conclusion with the closing chorus to "Hey Jude." Dozens of children, Sgt. Pepper's impersonators, and much of Live 8's lineup, including Pete Townshend, Floyd's Roger Waters, and Bob Geldof, joined Paul onstage. The show's conclusion was extraordinary, with or without U2.

The lineup in Paris consisted of Jamiroquai, Johnny Hallyday, and Placebo. Headliners in Rome consisted of Duran Duran, Faith

Hill, and Tim McGraw. Chris De Burgh, Audioslave, A-HA, and Green Day played in Berlin. The crew in Toronto consisted of Barenaked Ladies, Bruce Cockburn, Bryan Adams, Deep Purple, Run-D.M.C., Mötley Crüe, and Neil Young. Artists in Philadelphia included Stevie Wonder, Bon Jovi, the Dave Matthews Band, Def Leppard, Destiny's Child, Linkin Park playing with Jay-Z, Sarah McLachlan, and Will Smith.

Although the concerts were free, 66,500 pairs of tickets for the London concert were allocated in June to winners of a mobile-phone text-message competition. Entry into the contest involved listeners to breakfast shows on BBC and commercial radio stations sending the answer to a multiple choice question via a text message for a small fee. Winners of Live 8 tickets were randomly drawn from those who answered correctly with a one-in-twenty-eight chance of winning a pair of tickets. As a result of the millions of texts sent in during the competition, three million pounds was raised for charity organizations around the globe.

In Toronto, thirty-five thousand tickets were distributed in under twenty minutes. Many tickets showed up on the auction site eBay, upsetting organizers, such as Bob Geldof. At first, eBay was persistent in allowing its users to profit from Live 8 tickets, stating that there were no laws against their sale. The cyberspace company also promised to make a donation equaling what they would be making for such sales. Angered consumers ended up placing fake bids for the tickets. In time, eBay withdrew all its sales of Live 8 tickets per the request of the British government and the organizers, avoiding further controversy.

Funds raised beyond 1.6 million pounds were used "to pay for the costs of Live 8, as it is a free event," according to the Web site. An official Live 8 DVD set hit stores internationally in November 2005, one year after the release of the original Live Aid's four-disc DVD set in November 2004.

13

And in the End

THE MEGA-ENTERTAINMENT INDUSTRY as we see it and know it would not exist without the Beatles. Nothing can compare to their impact on the world. In their short careers together, the Beatles brought concept albums, psychedelia, society-altering tours, music videos, animated shorts, and godly poetry to the mass media. On the other hand, the united friendships making up U2 having been holding strong for well over a quarter century. As a cultural guide, and as a lobbyist, Bono has picked up his humanitarian efforts where Lennon left off. Rather than walking around naked, irritating world leaders, publicly disrespecting his bandmates, getting arrested for drug possession, and nearly being exiled from a powerful nation, Bono is on top of the game. The Irish statesman is shaking hands with President Bush, helping to earn millions for those in need. While John is the better icon when it comes to changing the world with music, Bono is an international hero.

Notions of Bono's next steps in his political career may include running for office. He has stated that his primary job is as an entertainer, but he may grow tired of being a rock star one day. It would not be inconceivable for him to make the transition from a public relations giant to a politician. In the 1980s, Clint Eastwood was the mayor of Carmel, California, and Ronald Reagan was the president of the United States. Sonny Bono was a congressman representing California in 1994, as well as mayor of Palm Springs, but lost the race for Senator. Professional wrestler and screen actor Jesse Ventura served as governor of Minnesota in the late '90s, and Arnold Schwarzenegger was sworn in as the thirty-eighth governor of California in 2003.

Is it fair to label U2 as "the Beatles of their Generation"? The general consensus is "no." The multitalented Little Steven Van Zandt, guitarist for Bruce Springsteen, host of an underground radio program, and wise-guy actor on *The Sopranos*, claims that the Beatles' sounds, looks, and attitudes cannot ever be reproduced. "There's just no equivalent to the Beatles today. Everything they brought to the table was new. It was revolutionary, as opposed to the twenty-first century's pop era. There can never be an equivalent to the Beatles."

Even Paul McCartney stated, "We were a good little band. . . . You have to admit we were fucking good."[1]

"How dare someone place U2 side-by-side with the Beatles, or Bono next to John Lennon," asked Blues Traveler front man, John Popper. "Lennon really shaped a generation. So did Bob Marley, Bob Dylan, and Jimi Hendrix. People always say to me that I can help shape a generation because I'm out there in a rock band and I'm in the merchandise. But a pop star is just another form of advertising unless he or she can actually do something that significantly changes the world with their music. John Lennon did that. And Bono, God bless him, is a fine singer and great songwriter, but he's nowhere near Lennon.

"The one thing I have to allow Bono is that enough time hasn't passed for us to appreciate his impact," Popper continued. "Based on what I know about music, Lennon brought classical music and composition to rock and roll with the help of the other Beatles. And it can't be replaced. Bono will be the first one to tell you that he is just a musician."

John Popper, *photo by Todd McFliker*

Both Paul and Ringo will almost undoubtedly cut new albums, film videos, and go on global tours. And the high-paying public will continue to support such ventures. However, the majority of consumers will only spend their hard-earned dollars on the artists' older material, such as the *Anthology* CDs and videos, as well as the *1* compilation. Biographical books and films will earn millions as well. Following such releases, Paul may regain his status as the richest cat in England, even after his second wife took him for numerous millions. On the other hand, U2 will continue to make gold records and sell out stadiums with fresh tunes, as they have been doing for over a quarter of a century. Regardless of which paths all of these icons choose for their futures, both the Beatles' and U2's music will continue to shine on, like the moon and the stars and the sun.

When a magazine reporter asked Bono in 2004 just how *does* one dismantle an atomic bomb, he replied with the Fab solution, "With love." Love *is* all you need.[2]

14

John and Bono
in Their
Own Words

John Lennon:

"Christianity will go. It will vanish and shrink. I needn't argue with that; I'm right and I will be proved right. We're more popular than Jesus now; I don't know which will go first, rock and roll or Christianity."[1]

"You have to be a bastard to make it, and that's a fact. And the Beatles are the biggest bastards on earth."[2]

"As usual, there is a great woman behind every idiot."[3]

"Guilt for being rich, and guilt thinking that perhaps love and peace isn't enough and you have to go and get shot or something."[4]

"I believe in everything until it's disproved. So I believe in fairies, the myths, dragons. It all exists, even if it's in your mind. Who's to say that dreams and nightmares aren't as real as the here and now?"[5]

"I believe in God, but not as one thing, not as an old man in the sky. I believe that what people call God is something in all of us. I believe that what Jesus and Mohammed and Buddha and all the rest said was right. It's just that the translations have gone wrong."6

"I don't intend to be a performing flea any more. I was the dream weaver, but although I'll be around I don't intend to be running at 20,000 miles an hour trying to prove myself. I don't want to die at 40."7

"I'm not going to change the way I look or the way I feel to conform to anything. I've always been a freak. So I've been a freak all my life and I have to live with that, you know. I'm one of those people."8

"If being an egomaniac means I believe in what I do and in my art or music, then in that respect you can call me that. . . . I believe in what I do, and I'll say it."9

"If everyone demanded peace instead of another television set, then there'd be peace."10

"If someone thinks that love and peace is a cliché that must have been left behind in the Sixties, that's his problem. Love and peace are eternal."11

"It was like being in the eye of a hurricane. You'd wake up in a concert and think, Wow, how did I get here?"12

"Music is everybody's possession. It's only publishers who think that people own it."13

"My role in society, or any artist's or poet's role, is to try and express what we all feel. Not to tell people how to feel. Not as a preacher, not as a leader, but as a reflection of us all."14

"Newspaper people have a habit of putting you in the front pages to sell their papers, and then after they've sold their papers and got big circulations, they say, 'Look at what we've done for you.'"[15]

"Our society is run by insane people for insane objectives. I think we're being run by maniacs for maniacal ends and I think I'm liable to be put away as insane for expressing that. That's what's insane about it."[16]

"The basic thing nobody asks is why do people take drugs of any sort? Why do we have these accessories to normal living to live? I mean, is there something wrong with society that's making us so pressurized, that we cannot live without guarding ourselves against it?"[17]

"The postman wants an autograph. The cab driver wants a picture. The waitress wants a handshake. Everyone wants a piece of you."[18]

"The thing the sixties did was to show us the possibilities and the responsibility that we all had. It wasn't the answer. It just gave us a glimpse of the possibility."[19]

"The worst drugs are as bad as anybody's told you. It's just a dumb trip, which I can't condemn people if they get into it, because one gets into it for one's own personal, social, emotional reasons. It's something to be avoided if one can help it."[20]

"We were all on this ship in the sixties, our generation, a ship going to discover the New World. And the Beatles were in the crow's nest of that ship."[21]

"You either get tired fighting for peace, or you die."[22]

Bono:

"Politically, I'm looking around, there's elections coming up all over the place, in England, in the US I'm sick and tired of party politics. You know, the left, the right. I'm sick of the left, I'm sick of the right. Even the liberals are giving me a pain in the ass. We need new solutions to new problems."[23]

"Everybody's trying to say, 'U2, the next this, the next that.' You get record industry people saying, 'As big as the Beatles.'"[24]

"U2's not a pop group. They are in this for real," said Lou Reed in 1987.[25]

"It's not how you play it, it's why you're playing it. Instruments are just bits of wood and metal nailed together, plastic skins stretched over boxes. It's what you do with them that's important."[26]

"The right to be ridiculous is something I hold very dear. Guilty of all that I'm charged with."[27]

"Who said decadence is not about living the life and having the finest wine and not tasting it? I think she called it the sweet aroma of spoiled opportunity."[28]

"Self-consciousness is never sexy. I mean, I've watched myself on TV, and I've just thought to myself, 'What an asshole.'"[29]

"I'll never forget one day during my Administration," explained Bill Clinton, "Secretary [Lawrence] Summers comes in and says, 'You know. Some guy just came in to see me in jeans and a T-shirt, and he just had one name, but he sure was smart.'"[30]

"Like Superman turning into Clark Kent, the earnest politician operative took over."[31]

"Bono is a pretty unique individual, and he's got great judgment," said Adam. "He's able to perform open-heart surgery and zap people with a bit of brain surgery at the same time."[32]

"Somebody once said to me, 'In America, you can only be famous for one thing at a time.' That's clearly not true in Bono's case," said U2 manager, Paul McGuiness.[33]

"I am Bono and I'm sick of him. I really am. . . . Like Van Morrison said, 'I'll be great when I'm finished.'"[34]

"The problem with voting is that no matter who you vote for, the government always gets in."[35]

"I think we weave God, sex, and politics together in a way that's very unusual in white music."[36]

"Our audiences are very smart, and if I abuse that relationship it would simply end. If I told people how to vote, they would tell me, 'Go Fuck Yourself.'"[37]

15

The Beatles and U2 Records

Beatles records in the United States

Let It Be, May 1970
Abbey Road, October 1969
Yellow Submarine, January 1969
The Beatles, a.k.a. "The White Album," November 1968
Magical Mystery Tour, November 1967
Sgt. Pepper's Lonely Hearts Club Band, June 1967
Revolver, August 1966
Rubber Soul, December 1965
Help! August 1965
Meet the Beatles! January 1964
Introducing the Beatles, January 1964

U2 records in the United States

How to Dismantle an Atomic Bomb, November 2004
All That You Can't Leave Behind, October 2000

The Best of 1980–1990, November 1998
Pop, March 1997
Zooropa, July 1993
Achtung Baby, November 1991
Rattle and Hum, October 1988
The Joshua Tree, March 1987
The Unforgettable Fire, October 1984
Under a Blood Red Sky, October 1983
War, March 1983
October, October 1981
Boy, October 1980

16

The Beatles and U2 Tour History

The Beatles on Tour

San Francisco – August 1965
Hollywood – August 1965
San Diego – August 1965
Portland – August 1965
Bloomington, IN – August 1965
Chicago – August 1965
Houston – August 1965
Atlanta – August 1965
Toronto – August 1965
New York City – August 1965
New York City – September 1964
Dallas – September 1964
Kansas City – September 1964
New Orleans – September 1964
Cleveland – September 1964
Pittsburgh – September 1964

Baltimore – September 1964
Boston – September 1964
Jacksonville – September 1964
Montreal – September 1964
Toronto – September 1964
Detroit – September 1964
Chicago – September 1964
Milwaukee – September 1964
Indianapolis – September 1964
Philadelphia – September 1964
Atlantic City – August 1964
New York City – August 1964
Cincinnati – August 1964
Denver – August 1964
Hollywood – August 1964
Vancouver – August 1964
Seattle – August 1964
Las Vegas – August 1964
San Francisco – August 1964
Miami – February 1964
New York City – February 1964
Washington, DC – February 1964
New York City – *The Ed Sullivan Show* – February 1964

U2 Tour History

Vertigo 2005 World Tour

March 28th San Diego, CA – Sports Arena
March 30th San Diego, CA – Sports Arena
April 1st Anaheim, CA – Arrowhead Pond
April 2nd Anaheim, CA – Arrowhead Pond
April 5th Los Angeles, CA – Staples Center
April 6th Los Angeles, CA – Staples Center
April 9th San Jose, CA – HP Pavilion
April 10th San Jose, CA – HP Pavilion
April 14th Phoenix, AZ – Glendale Arena

April 15th Phoenix, AZ – Glendale Arena
April 20th Denver, CO – Pepsi Center
April 21st Denver, CO – Pepsi Center
April 24th Seattle, WA – Key Arena
April 25th Seattle, WA – Key Arena
April 28th Vancouver, BC – General Motors Place
April 29th Vancouver, BC – General Motors Place
May 7th & May 9th Chicago, IL – United Center
May 10th Chicago, IL – United Center
May 12th Chicago, IL – United Center
May 14th Philadelphia, PA – Wachovia Center
May 22nd Philadelphia, PA – Wachovia Center
May 17 & May 18 East Rutherford, NJ – Continental Airlines Arena
May 21 New York, NY – Madison Square Garden
May 24 Boston, MA – Fleet Center
May 26 Boston, MA – Fleet Center
May 28 Boston, MA – Fleet Center

European Dates
June 10th Brussels – King Baudouin Stadium
June 12th Gelsenkirchen – Schalke Stadium
June 14th Manchester – City of Manchester Stadium
June 15th Manchester – City of Manchester Stadium
June 18th London – Twickenham Stadium
June 19th London – Twickenham Stadium
June 21st Glasgow – Hampden Park
June 24th Dublin – Croke Park
June 25th Dublin – Croke Park
June 29th Cardiff – Millenium Stadium
July 2nd Vienna – Ernst Happel Stadium
July 5th Katowice – Slaski Stadium
July 7th Berlin – Olympic Stadium
July 9th Paris – Stade de France
July 10th Paris – Stade de France
July 13th Amsterdam – Arena
July 15th Amsterdam – Arena

July 16th Amsterdam – Arena
July 18th Zurich – Letzigrund Stadium
July 21st Milan – San Siro
July 23rd Rome – Olympic Stadium
July 27th Oslo – Vallehovin Stadium
July 29th Gothenburg – Ullevi Stadium
July 31st Copenhagen – Parken
August 3rd Munich – Olympic Stadium
August 5th Nice – Parc des Sports Charles Ehrmann
August 7th Barcelona – Camp Nou
August 9th San Sebastian – Anoeta Stadium
August 11th Madrid – Estadio Vicente Calderon
August 14th Lisbon – Alvalade

North America Fall 2005 Tour Dates

September 12th Toronto – Air Canada Centre
September 14th Toronto – Air Canada Centre
September 20th Chicago – United Center
September 21st Chicago – United Center
September 23rd Minneapolis – Target Center
September 25th Milwaukee – Bradley Center
October 3rd Boston – Fleet Center
October 4th Boston – Fleet Center
October 7th New York – Madison Square Garden
October 8th New York – Madison Square Garden
October 10th New York – Madison Square Garden
October 16th Philadelphia – Wachovia Center
October 17th Philadelphia – Wachovia Center
October 19th Washington – DC MCI Center
October 20th Washington – DC MCI Center
October 22nd Pittsburgh – Mellon Arena
October 24th Detroit – Palace of Auburn Hills
October 28th Houston – Toyota Center
October 29th Dallas – American Airlines Center
November 1st Los Angeles – Staples Center
November 2nd Los Angeles – Staples Center

November 13th Miami – American Airlines Arena
November 16th Tampa – St. Pete Times Forum
November 18th Atlanta – Philips Arena
November 25th Ottawa – Corel Centre
November 26th Montreal – Bell Centre
December 7th Hartford – Civic Center
December 9th Buffalo – HSBC Arena
December 10th Cleveland – Gund Arena
December 14th St. Louis – Savvis Center
December 15th Omaha – Qwest Center
December 17th Salt Lake City – Delta Center
December 19th Portland – Rose Garden

Tours

Elevation 2001 (3rd leg) autumn, North America October–
   November 2001
Elevation 2001 (2nd leg) summer, Europe July–August 2001
Elevation 2001 (1st leg) spring, North America March–June 2001
PopMart tour (5th leg) Australia, Japan, and South Africa
   February–March 1998
PopMart tour (4th leg) South America January–February 1998
PopMart tour (3rd leg) North America October–December 1997
PopMart tour (2nd leg) Europe July–September 1997
PopMart tour 97 (1st leg) North America April–July 1997
Zoo TV tour Zoomerang, New Zooland, ZOO TV Japan
   November–December 1993
Zoo TV tour Zooropa '93 Europe May–August 1993
Zoo TV tour – Outside Broadcast (3rd leg) North America
   August–November 1992
Zoo TV tour (2nd leg) Europe May–June 1992
Zoo TV tour (1st leg) North America February–April 1992
The Lovetown tour (2nd leg) Europe November–January 1990
The Lovetown tour (1st leg) New Zealand, Australia, and Japan
   September–December 1989
The Joshua Tree tour (3rd leg) America September–November 1987
The Joshua Tree tour (2nd leg) Europe May–August 1987

The Joshua Tree tour (1st leg) America April–May 1987
Amnesty International's "Conspiracy of Hope" tour June–June 1986
The Unforgettable Fire tour (4th leg) North America February–
    May 1985
The Unforgettable Fire tour (3rd leg) Europe January–
    February 1985
The Unforgettable Fire tour (2nd leg) North America–
    December 1984
The Under Australian Skies tour – the Unforgettable Fire tour
    (1st leg) New Zealand, Australia, and Europe August–
    November 1984
The War tour (2nd leg) North America, European Festivals,
    and Japan April–November 1983
The War tour (1st leg) UK & Europe February–April 1983
Pre-War tour December–December 1982
European Dates/Festival May–August 1982
October tour (3rd leg) America February–March 1982
October tour (2nd leg) North America & Europe November–
    January 1982
October tour (1st leg) Europe October–November 1981
The Boy tour (2nd leg) America and Europe December–
    February 1981
The Boy tour (1st leg) UK and Europe September–
    November 1980
11 O'Clock Tick Tock tour UK and Ireland May–July 1980
U2–3 London tours December–December 1979
Irish tour and London dates December–March 1980
Irish tours March–October 1979

Notes

2. The Beatles' Revolution

1. The Beatles, *The Beatles Anthology* (San Francisco: Chronicle Books, 2000), 134.
2. Ibid., 144.
3. Ibid., 146.
4. David Fricke, "Beatlemania," *Rolling Stone* 942 (2004): 51.
5. Bill Harry, *The British Invasion: How the Beatles and Other UK Bands Conquered America* (Surrey, England: Chrome Dreams Publishing, 2004), 12.
6. Ibid.
7. Ibid., 14.
8. Ibid., 34.
9. Karlene Faith, *The Long Prison Journey of Leslie Van Houten* (Boston: Northeastern University Press, 2001), 106.
10. Nuel Emmons, *Manson in His Own Words* (New York: Grove Press, 1986), 103.
11. Jess Bravin, *Squeaky* (New York: Buzz Books, 1997), 126.
12. Ronald L. Davis, *A History of Music in American Life Volume III* (Malabar, FL: Robert Kreiger Publishing Company, 1981), 390.
13. "The Beatles and The Who," in *LIFE Rock & Roll at 50* (New York: Time-Life Publishing, 2002), 14.
14. Leonard Michaels, "The Violent Gods," *Rolling Stone* 415 (1984): 68.

15. Chris Welch, *Led Zeppelin—Dazed and Confused* (New York: Thunder's Mouth Press, 1998), 8.

3. U2: Four People, Four Individuals, Four Friends

1. Robert Hilburn, "Imagine if John Lennon had lived to be 60," *Los Angeles Times*, Pro Quest: http://lynnlang.student.lynn.edu:2053/pqdweb? index=1&di d=65053326&SrchMode=1&sid=4&Fmt=3& VInst=PROD&VType=PQD&RQT=309&VName=PQD&TS=110 892030303&clientId=9094; accessed spring 2005.
2. *Out of Ireland*, directed by Jim Sheridan (Eagle Vision USA, 2003).
3. Scott Isler, "Operation Uplift" in *The U2 Reader*, ed. Hank Bordounte (New York: Hal Leonard Corporation, 1983), 13.
4. Bill Flanagan, *U2 at the End of the World* (New York: Dell Publishing, 1996), 8.
5. Chuck Klosterman, "Mysterious Days," *Spin* 20, No. 12 (2004): 62.
6. Anthony De Curtis, "Raw Power," *Revolver,* no. 3 (2000): 86.
7. Flanagan, 9.
8. Paul Rees, "Riders on the Storm," *Q* 220 (2004): 73.
9. David Fricke, "The 100 Greatest Guitarists of All Time" in *Rolling Stone* 931 (2003): 56.
10. Ibid., 57.
11. Niall Stokes, *Into the Heart* (New York: Thunder's Mouth Press, 2002), 7.
12. Unknown, *Dublin Boys Tops of Pops!* in Bordowitz, *The U2 Reader*, 2–3.
13. Paulo Hewitt, "Getting Into U2," in Bordowitz, *The U2 Reader*, 7.
14. Ibid., 4.
15. Pimm Jal de la Parra, *U2 Live* (New York: Omnibus Press, 2003), 17.
16. Tim Sommer, "U2," in Bordowitz, *The U2 Reader*, 10.
17. Isler, 15.
18. Stokes, 41.
19. Ibid., 37
20. De Curtis, 85.
21. Ethlie Ann Vare, "U2: At War With Mediocrity" in Bordowitz, *The U2 Reader*, 22.
22. Stokes, 37.
23. Alan Crandall, "500 Greatest Songs of All Time," *Rolling Stone* 963 (2004): 58.

24. Steve Turner, *A Hard Day's Write* (New York: Harper Collins Publishers, 1999), 147.
25. De La Parra, 48.
26. Ibid., 52.
27. Flanagan, 49.
28. De Curtis, 85.
29. de la Parra, 79
30. Stokes, 62.
31. Deborah Sussman, "U2," in Bordowitz, *The U2 Reader*, 36.
32. William C. Trott, "America's Sexiest Men," in Bordowitz, *The U2 Reader*, 37.
33. Stokes, 93.
34. Ted Mico, "Hating U2," *Spin* Vol 4, no. 10 (1989), 25: 76.
35. Flanagan, 14, 28.
36. De Curtis, 86.
37. Stephen Dalton, "Achtung Stations," *Uncut* 90 (2004): 52.
38. Flanagan, 22.
39. Ibid, 31.
40. De Curtis, 85.
41. Josh Tyrangiel, "Can Bono Save the World?" *Time* 159, no. 9. (2001): 64.
42. Todd McFliker, "U2: All That You Can't Live Without," *RAG Magazine*, November 2001, 24.
43. Tyrangiel, 64.
44. Fricke, 62.
45. Rees, 74.
46. Flanagan, 12.
47. Mico, 76.

5. Records of a Generation: *Sgt. Pepper's* vs. *Achtung Baby*

1. Pat Blashill, "500 Greatest Albums of All Time," *Rolling Stone* 937 (2003): 92.
2. Elvis Costello, "The Beatles," *Rolling Stone* 946 (2004): 85.
3. Blashill, 85.
4. Stokes, 97.
5. Keith Badman, *The Beatles Off the Record* (New York: Omnibus Press, 2001), 256, 258.

6. Diana Scrimgeour, *U2 Show* (New York: Riverhead Books, 2004), 279.
7. Stephen Dalton, "Achtung Stations," *Uncut* 90 (2004): 52.
8. Harrison in Turner, 117.
9. Dalton, 56.
10. Ibid., 52.
11. Stokes, 95.
12. Ibid.
13. Blashill, 92.
14. Stokes, 103.
15. Badman, 256.
16. Turner, 121.
17. Badman, 256.
18. Turner, 118.
19. Dalton, 52.
20. Turner, 118.
21. Ibid., 122.
22. The Edge quoted in Stokes, 100.
23. Ibid., 104.
24. Turner, 130.
25. Badman, 263.
26. Turner, 122.
27. Ibid., 118, 134.
28. Badman, 257.
29. Ibid, 263.
30. Greg Kot, "Eight Days a Week," *Rolling Stone* 863 (2001): 35.
31. Anthony De Curtis, "Help," *Rolling Stone* 863 (2001): 36.
32. Kot, 58.
33. Jon Pareles, "Hello, Goodbye," *Rolling Stone* 863 (2001): 58.
34. Tom Moon, "Something," *Rolling Stone* 863 (2001): 58.

6. Concerts of a Generation

1. Michael Bracewell, "U2 and Rock Music as Spectacle," in Scrimgeour, *U2 Show.*
2. Scrimgeour, 154.
3. Larry Kane, *Ticket to Ride* (New York: Penguin Books, 2004), 7.
4. McFliker, 24.
5. Badman, 125.

6. Charles Watson, "Rock Music," in *Microsoft Encarta Online Encyclopedia 2004,* http://encarta.msn.com/ encyclopedia_7 61558548/Rock_Music. html, accessed December 10, 2004.

7. Kane, 105.

8. Badman, 85.

9. Ibid.

10. McFliker, 25.

11. Nick Marino, "U2 March 24, 2001," *Spin* 17, no. 6 (2001): 58.

12. Jal De La Parra, 229.

13. McFliker, 24.

14. Kane, 102.

15. Ibid., 72.

16. McFliker, 28.

17. Kane, 102.

18. Ibid., 31.

19. Ibid., 102.

20. Badman, 87.

7.   Films of a Generation

1. Noel Gallagher, "The 101 Greatest Beatles Songs," *MOJO,* July 2006, 121.

8.   Rock Star: The Cultural Icon

1. Paul Theroux, "Why We Loved the Beatles," *Rolling Stone* 415 (February 16, 1984): 21.

2. Angus Batey, "Fly Guy," in *MOJO Icons,* (London: Mappin House, 2005), 121.

3. Ibid., 138.

4. James Henke, "'The Edge' the *Rolling Stone* interview," *Rolling Stone* 521 (March 1988): 53.

5. Klosterman, 64.

6. Vare, 24.

7. Anthony De Curtis, "Truths and Consequences," *Rolling Stone* May 7, 1987, 28.

8. Steve Sutherland, "We're More Popular Than Jesus Now," *Uncut,* February 2006, 50.

9. John Muncie, "The Beatles and the Spectacle of Youth," in *The Beatles, Popular Music and Society*, ed. Ian Inglis (London: Palgrave, 2000), 36.

10. Wenner, 34.
11. Elizabeth Thomson and David Gutman, *The Lennon Companion* (New York: Schirmer Books, 1987), 5.

9. Rock Star: The Political Icon

1. Lionel Tiger, "Why, It Was Fun!" *Rolling Stone* 415 (February 1984): 28.
2. Jan Wiener, *Come Together, John Lennon in His Time* (Chicago: University of Illinois Press, 1991), 97.
3. Ibid., 53.
4. Mikal Gilmore, "Lennon Lives Forever" *Rolling Stone* 989 (December 2005): 64.
5. De Curtis, 54–57.
6. Mico, 35–36.
7. De Curtis, 60.
8. Chuck Klosterman, "April 1990," *Spin* 22, no. 4 (2006): 100.
9. Richard Blow, "Bono Turns Up the Political Heat," *George,* April 2000, 64.
10. Tyrangiel, 64.
11. Ibid., 69.
12. Rees, 74.
13. James Traub, "The Statesman." *The New York Times Magazine*, 2005, 10.
14. Jesse Helms, "Bono," *Time* 167, no. 19 (2006): 104.

11. The Beatles and U2 for Sale

1. Walter Everett, *The Beatles as Musicians* (New York: Oxford University Press, 1999), 286–87.
2. Du Noyer, 31.
3. "U2 About Bootlegs," U2 Bootlegs, www.u2bootlegs.nl, accessed Summer 2006.
4. Ibid.
5. Evan Serpick, "The iTunes Holdouts." *Rolling Stone* 1004/1005 (2006): 22.
6. Cynthia Lennon, *John* (New York: Random House Large Print, 2005) 384.
7. Ibid., 409.
8. Julian Lennon, *John* (New York: Random House Large Print, 2005), xii.
9. Larry Kane, *Lennon Revealed* (Philadelphia: Running Press, 2005), 38.

10. Ibid, 95.
11. Geoffrey Giuliano, *Blackbird: The Life and Times of Paul McCartney* (New York: Dutton, 1991), 23.
12. Ibid., 131.
13. Ibid., 236.
14. Ibid., 318.
15. George Harrison, *I Me Mine* (San Francisco: Chronicle Books, 2002), 33.
16. Ibid., 43.
17. Alan Clayson, *Ringo Starr: Straight Man or Joker* (New York: Paragon House, 1992), 252.
18. Ibid., 242.
19. Yoko Ono, *Memories of John Lennon* (New York: HarperCollins Publishing, 2005), ix.
20. Ibid., 27.
21. Ibid., 215.
22. Ibid., 252
23. Dave Thompson, *Bono: In His Own Words* (New York: Omnibus Press, 1989), 60.
24. Ibid., 11.
25. Michka Assayas, *Bono in Conversation with Michka Assayas* (New York: Penguin, 2005), ix.
26. Ibid., 38.
27. Paul McCartney, *Paul McCartney Paintings* (Bulfinch Press: Boston, 2000), 53.
28. Ibid., 9.
29. Ibid., 52.
30. John Lennon, *Real Love: The Drawings for Sean* (New York: Random House, 1999), 3.

12. The Icons Come Together: Live 8 with a Little Help from Some Friends

1. Henke, 100.

13. And in the End

1. Danny Eccleston, "Am I a Beatles Fan or What," *MOJO* 152 (2006): 86.
2. Adrian Deevoy, "U2 Walk on Water," *Blender*, November 2004, 120.

14. John and Bono in Their Own Words

1. John Lennon quoted in Sutherland, 50.
2. *John Lennon Quotes,* Brainy Quotes, www.brainyquote.com/quotes/authors/ j/john_lennon.html, accessed Summer 2006.
3. Ibid.
4. Ibid.
5. Ibid.
6. Ibid.
7. Ibid.
8. Ibid.
9. Ibid.
10. Ibid.
11. Ibid.
12. Ibid.
13. Ibid.
14. Ibid.
15. Ibid.
16. Ibid.
17. Ibid.
18. Ibid.
19. Ibid.
20. Ibid.
21. Ibid.
22. Ibid.
23. De Curtis, 60.
24. Ibid, 28.
25. Jay Cocks, "Band on the Run," *Time* 129, no. 17 (1987): 75.
26. Isler, 12.
27. Rees, 74.
28. Deevoy, 116.
29. Klosterman (2004), 68.
30. Tyrangiel, 64.
31. Ibid.
32. Ibid., 69.
33. Fricke, 58.
34. Deevoy, 118.
35. Rees, 76.
36. Klosterman, 100.

37. Klosterman, 68.
38. Blow, 64.
39. De Curtis, 60.

Index

This index was designed to assist readers in quickly locating important information, broken down into eight categories: Albums, Artwork & Photography, Culture Changing Events, Landmarks, Movies, Organizations, People & Bands, and Books & Periodicals.

BOOKS & PERIODICALS